Peyton Manning:

Passing the Record

INDY-TECH

PUBLISHING

International Standard Book Number: 0-7906-1314-X

Chief Executive Officer:	Alan Symons
President:	Scott Weaver
Chief Operating Officer:	Richard White
Acquisitions Editor:	Brad Schepp
Editorial Assistant:	Dana Eaton
Cover Design:	Robin Roberts
Copyeditor:	Linda White
Research:	Dana Eaton
Game Recaps and Statistics:	Richard White
Pagination Editor:	Kim Heusel
Illustrations, Photos, & Drawings:	Associated Press unless otherwise noted, with proper permissions obtained.
Cover Photo:	Associated press, with proper permissions obtained

Printed in the USA, at Ripon Community Printers, Ripon WI.

Table of Contents

Peyton Manning

The 2004-2005 Season

Peyton Manning's goal for the 2004 season was to win the Super Bowl. Until game 6, nobody was talking about Dan Marino's 1984 record for most touchdown passes in a season. It was in game 6 that Manning's touchdown passes equaled that of Marino's at the same point in the season. From that game on, all of the talk was about how soon Manning would break the record and by how much.

The Colts had little trouble scoring this season and Manning threw more touchdowns than Marino did. Manning averaged 2.88 touchdown passes per game, and if you exclude the final regular season game against Denver when he played only the opening 3-play drive, his average was just over 3 per game. He threw 7 touchdown passes against the Houston Texans and 6 against the Detroit Lions. Manning tossed the ball into the end zone 5 times against 4 other teams. The final game against Denver is the only game without a Manning touchdown pass.

The defense was criticized for much of the season, ranking near the bottom of the NFL in yards allowed. However, they ranked near the top of the league in other important defensive catego-ries. When the offense scores multiple times in the first half, the defense will naturally fall off in the 2nd half, allowing the other team to use up the clock and reduce their opportunities to score.

As Manning threw touchdowns, the Colts won more and more games, going 12-4 on the season, with one of those losses be-ing their final regular season game in Denver, when Manning completed 3 plays in the opening drive before Jim Sorgi took over. The Colts had a streak of 4 games when they scored over 40 points.

Manning "spread the wealth", completing touchdown passes to 6 different receivers. The Colts became the 1st team in the NFL to have 3 receivers with 10 or more touchdown recep-tions in a season. Five players caught 5 or more touchdown passes from Manning. Manning's touchdown passes were spread fairly evenly across the first 3 quarters of each game. In many games, Jim Sorgi played the 4th quarter. Manning tossed 31 touch-down passes from the "red zone" within the 20-yard line. His proficiency in passing and his mastery of the Colts' offensive tactics helped him to move the ball quickly toward the end zone, providing opportunities for the Colts. Manning threw 32 of his touchdowns indoors and 26 of those at the RCA Dome.

As the season progressed, the media and many fans focused more on "the record" and less on winning. In the December 19 game against Baltimore, Colts fans were disappointed when Manning elected to end the game by running out the clock in-stead of attempting to tie "the record". For Manning and the Colts, the season was about winning, not setting records. The fans understood that later, but in the heat of the moment they wanted to see "the record" tied on their home field. Manning tied and broke the record against San Diego, in front of his home crowd at the RCA Dome on December 26, 2004. His passes to James Mungro (tie) and Brandon Stokley (the record) are passes that will go down in history.

Manning talked little about "the record" during the season, focusing on the Colts winning and going to the Super Bowl. It was not until the game against San Diego that we finally saw Manning relax, smile, and talk about breaking Dan Marino's record. In the postgame interviews following that game, Manning talked live with Marino, whom he described as one of his idols. Manning was more talkative about the record after that game, but quickly brought his attention, and the attention of the Colts, back to winning games and getting to the Super Bowl.

Manning threw for 4,557 yards, 3rd in the NFL for the season. His Quarterback Rating was the highest in the history of the league at 121.1 and Manning was awarded the Associated Press NFL Most Valuable Player Award for the 2nd consecutive year.

The Colts moved into the postseason, defeating Denver at the RCA Dome but losing to New England in Foxboro. Manning performed superbly in the game against Denver, throwing 4 touchdown passes. The Patriots outplayed the Colts in Foxboro, holding the Colts to just 3 points.

It was a season of memories for Colts fans all over the world. Watching Peyton Manning chase Dan Marino's record was a joy and created a great deal of excitement for almost everyone who enjoys football. Manning's 2004 season is one he will always remember, as will his fans. Peyton Manning will go down in history as one of the most effective and exciting quarterbacks in the NFL.

The Touchdowns 2004

#	Date	Opponent	Yards	Who
1	9/9	New England	3	Harrison
2	9/9	New England	7	Stokley
3	9/19	Tennessee	5	Wayne
4	9/19	Tennessee	1	Pollard
5	9/26	Green Bay	36	Wayne
6	9/26	Green Bay	28	Harrison
7	9/26	Green Bay	34	Stokley
8	9/26	Green Bay	27	Stokley
9	9/26	Green Bay	1	Mungro
10	10/3	Jacksonville	15	Harrison
11	10/3	Jacksonville	16	Pollard
12	10/10	Oakland	1	Mungro
13	10/10	Oakland	35	Wayne
14	10/10	Oakland	4	Clark
15	10/24	Jacksonville	7	Harrison
16	10/24	Jacksonville	17	Clark
17	10/24	Jacksonville	9	Harrison
18	10/31	Kansas City	52	Harrison
19	10/31	Kansas City	5	Pollard
20	10/31	Kansas City	22	Harrison
21	10/31	Kansas City	41	Wayne
22	10/31	Kansas City	6	Wayne
23	11/8	Minnesota	5	Wayne
24	11/8	Minnesota	10	Pollard
25	11/8	Minnesota	4	Clark
26	11/8	Minnesota	19	Pollard
27	11/14	Houston	4	Stokley
28	11/14	Houston	5	Wayne
29	11/14	Houston	1	Clark

30	11/14	Houston	69		Stokley
31	11/14	Houston	80		Clark
32	11/21	Chicago	14		Pollard
33	11/21	Chicago	35		Wayne
34	11/21	Chicago	10		Harrison
35	11/21	Chicago	27		Wayne
36	11/25	Detroit	4		Stokley
37	11/25	Detroit	12		Stokley
38	11/25	Detroit	25		Stokley
39	11/25	Detroit	13		Harrison
40	11/25	Detroit	10		Harrison
41	11/25	Detroit	5		Harrison
42	12/5	Tennessee	24		Harrison
43	12/5	Tennessee	28		Stokley
44	12/5	Tennessee	10		Wayne
45	12/12	Houston	3		Harrison
46	12/12	Houston	12		Wayne
47	12/19	Baltimore	29		Harrison
48	12/26	**San Diego**	3		**Mungro***
49	12/26	**San Diego**	21		**Stokley****

* ties record
** breaks record

9

Peyton Manning

A Brief Biography

#18 Peyton Manning
Position: QB
Height: 6'5"
Weight: 230
Born: 03/24/1976 in New Orleans
College: Tennessee
Drafted: By Indianapolis Colts, #1 pick in 1st round.
NFL Experience: 7
Resides: Indianapolis IN

Peyton Manning was born to Archie and Olivia Manning March 24, 1976 in New Orleans, Louisiana. His father, Archie, was an NFL quarterback, playing for the New Orleans Saints. Peyton has two siblings: older brother Cooper and younger brother Eli, who is a quarterback for the New York Giants.

Manning grew up in the Garden District of New Orleans, with neighbors such as Novelist Anne Rice and Trent Reznor of the rock group Nine Inch Nails. He attended Isidore Newman High School and currently resides in Indianapolis.

Manning majored in Speech Communications and graduated from the University of Tennessee after attending high school in New Orleans. He was runner-up for the Heisman Trophy his senior year after passing for 3,819 yards and 36 touchdowns.

Manning was drafted by the Indianapolis Colts in 1998 and married his college sweetheart, Ashley Thompson, in 2001. His career with the Colts has been one of continued success, leading the Colts both on the field and off, compiling an impressive list of football accomplishments. He's also remained involved with his community.

In fact, Peyton Manning gives back to his community like few other athletes. With multiple events each year to help children and others in need, he founded the PeyBack Foundation in 1999 to help disadvantaged youth and to teach leadership skills. He has received many awards and gives as much as he can to his fans.

Passing Statistics

Year	Team	G	GS	Att	Comp	Pct	Yds	YPA	Lg	TD	Int
1998	Colts	16	16	575	326	56.7	3739	6.50	78	26	28
1999	Colts	16	16	533	331	62.1	4135	7.76	80	26	15
2000	Colts	16	16	571	357	62.5	4413	7.73	78	33	15
2001	Colts	16	16	547	343	62.7	4131	7.55	86	26	23
2002	Colts	16	16	591	392	66.3	4200	7.11	69	27	19
2003	Colts	16	16	566	379	67.0	4267	7.54	79	29	10
2004	Colts	16	16	497	336	67.6	4557	9.17	80	49	10
Total		112	112	3880	2464	63.5	29442	7.59	86	216	120

2004 Season Statistics

Season Schedule

Week	Date	Opponent	Results
1	9/9/04	New England	L 24-27
2	9/19/04	Tennessee	W 31-17
3	9/26/04	Green Bay	W 45-31
4	10/3/04	Jacksonville	W 24-17
5	10/10/04	Oakland	W 35-14
6	10/17/04	Bye week	
7	10/24/04	Jacksonville	L 24-27
8	10/31/04	Kansas City	L 35-45
9	11/8/04	Minnesota	W 31-28
10	11/14/04	Houston	W 49-14
11	11/21/04	Chicago	W 41-10
12	11/25/04	Detroit	W 41-9
13	12/5/04	Tennessee	W 51-24
14	12/12/04	Houston	W 23-14
15	12/19/04	Baltimore	W 20-10
16	12/26/04	San Diego	W 34-31 OT
17	1/2/05	Denver	L 14-33
Playoffs			
	1/9/05	Denver	W 49-24
	1/16/05	New England	L 3-20

Passing the Record

Dan Marino, Miami Dolphins	1984	Peyton Manning, Indianapolis Colts	2004
Opponent	TD	Opponent	TD
Washington	5	New England	2
New England	2	Tennessee	2
Buffalo	3	Green Bay	5
Indianapolis	2	Jacksonville	2
St. Louis	3	Oakland	3
Pittsburgh	2	Jacksonville	3
Houston	3	Kansas City	5
New England	4	Minnesota	4
Buffalo	3	Houston	5
New York	2	Chicago	4
Philadelphia	1	Detroit	6
San Diego	2	Tennessee	3
New York	4	Houston	2
Los Angeles	4	Baltimore	1
Indianapolis	4	**San Diego**	2
Dallas	4	Denver	0
Season Total	48	Season Total	49

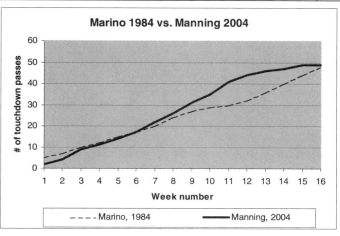

13

Summary of Touchdown Passes

By Quarter

1st Quarter: 14
2nd Quarter: 16
3rd Quarter: 12
4th Quarter: 7

Indoor vs. Outdoor

Indoor: 32
Outdoor: 17

By Receiver

Harrison: 14
(+ 1 from Sorgi)
Wayne: 11
(+ 1 from Sorgi)
Stokley: 10
Pollard: 6
Clark: 5
Mungro: 3

The 2004 Indianapolis Colts became the 1st team in NFL history to have 3 receivers with 10 or more touchdown receptions in a single season. They also had 5 receivers with 5 or more touchdown receptions.

Home vs. Away

Home: 26
Away: 23

By Yardage

1-9 yards: 19
10-19 yards: 12
20-29 yards: 9
30-39 yards: 5
40-49 yards: 1
50-59 yards: 1
60-69 yards: 1
70-79 yards: 0
80-89 yards: 1
90-100 yards: 0

By Team

New England: 2
Tennessee: 5
Green Bay: 5
Jacksonville: 5
Oakland: 3
Kansas City: 5
Minnesota: 4
Houston: 7
Chicago: 4
Detroit: 6
Baltimore: 1
San Diego: 2
Denver: 0

Punts vs. Touchdown Passes

Peyton Manning Touchdown Passes: 49
Hunter Smith Punts: 54
Ratio: 10 punts to every 9 touchdown passes.

This statistic is important in that Daunte Culpepper of the Minnesota Vikings ranked 2nd in the NFL in touchdown passes this season with 39, while his punter, Darren Bennett had 57 punts. Ratio: 10 punts for every 7 touchdown passes. Going into the final game in which Peyton Manning played only 3 downs, Hunter Smith had 48 punts to Manning's 49 touchdown passes!

Quarterback Rating

Peyton Manning also set a new NFL record for quarterback rating with a final rating of 121.1, breaking Steve Young's 1994 rating of 112.8. Peyton Manning had a total of 4,557 yards passing for the regular season, going 336 for 497 with 10 interceptions. This was yet another record that many NFL fans, historians, and commentators didn't believe would ever be broken.

Team Touchdown Record

Manning's 49 touchdown passes coupled with 2 by Jim Sorgi in the final game set an NFL record for most passing touchdowns by a team in a single season, breaking the 1984 record of 49 set by the Miami Dolphins.

Other Awards

Manning was awarded the Associated Press NFL Most Valuable Player award for 2004 and was also named the starting quarterback for the February 13, 2005 NFL Pro Bowl.

Game 1

Indianapolis Colts @
New England Patriots
September 9, 2004

Game Summary

In a rematch of the 2003 AFC Championship, Peyton Manning unknowingly started his march toward a record-breaking season. With two touchdown passes, no one is even thinking about Dan Marino's 1984 season of 48 touchdown passes. Manning passes the 25,000-yard mark in his 95th game, the second fastest to the 25,000-yard level, behind Dan Marino, who reached it in 92 games.

The Patriots open the game with a 32-yard field goal capping a 48-yard drive. Indianapolis moves from its own 28-yard line to the New England 6, before Tedy Bruschi picks off a Peyton Manning pass. New England moves just 20 yards before having to punt, where the Colts regain their momentum at the Indianapolis 37-yard line.

Manning uses the no-huddle offense to move the Colts back up the field, and the drive takes them into the beginning of the 2nd quarter of play, when Mike Vanderjagt evens the score with a 32-yard field goal. The game is tied 3-3. New England then goes "4 and out" and the Colts start their drive from their own 34-yard line. Nine plays later, Manning hands off to Dominic Rhodes for a 3-yard touchdown run. COLTS 10, PATRIOTS 3.

After a 20-yard return on the Vanderjagt kickoff, New England moves the ball up the field in short order, capping the drive with a 16-yard touchdown pass from Tom Brady to Deion Branch. The 75-yard drive was just 8 plays and ran less than 5 minutes off the clock. Indianapolis comes right back with a 7-play, 82-yard drive fueled by the passing of Peyton Manning. 2:22 later, Manning connects with Marvin

Harrison for a 3-yard touchdown pass (**Manning's first of the season**). COLTS 17, PATRIOTS 10.

With just 42 seconds left in the first half, Brady leads the Patriots down the field, ending the half with an Adam Vinatieri 43-yard field goal. COLTS 17, PATRIOTS 13.

The second half opens with the Colts going "4 and out" and a Hunter Smith punt. New England returns the ball up the field, finishing the 69-yard drive with a Brady touchdown pass to David Patten from the 25-yard line. COLTS 17, PATRIOTS 20.

After an Edgerrin James fumble on the New England 18, the Patriots go 82 yards to score on an 8-yard pass from Brady to Daniel Graham. COLTS 17, PATRIOTS 27. The Colts drive right back, going 74 yards and into the 4th quarter, with Manning connecting with Brandon Stokley for a 7-yard touchdown strike (**Manning's 2nd of the season**). COLTS 24, PATRIOTS 27.

The remainder of the 4th quarter sees the two teams exchanging possessions, with Indianapolis having one final chance to score with 24 seconds on the clock. The Vanderjagt 48-yard field goal attempt is wide right, and the Patriots take over possession of the ball to end the game. It is Vanderjagt's first miss in 42 attempts.

COLTS 24, PATRIOTS 27 — FINAL

Peyton Manning — 2 touchdown passes

Passing the Record

Dan Marino, Miami Dolphins	1984	Peyton Manning, Indianapolis Colts	2004
Opponent	TD	*Opponent*	TD
Washington	5	New England	2
New England		Tennessee	
Buffalo		Green Bay	
Indianapolis		Jacksonville	
St. Louis		Oakland	
Pittsburgh		Jacksonville	
Houston		Kansas City	
New England		Minnesota	
Buffalo		Houston	
New York		Chicago	
Philadelphia		Detroit	
San Diego		Tennessee	
New York		Houston	
Los Angeles		Baltimore	
Indianapolis		San Diego	
Dallas		Denver	
Through 1 Game	**5**	**Through 1 Game**	**2**

Scoring Summary

Box Score

Team ↓ Quarter →	1	2	3	4	Score
Indianapolis	0	17	0	7	24
New England	3	10	14	0	27

Indianapolis

2nd Quarter:	32-yard field goal (Vanderjagt).
	3-yard touchdown run (Rhodes), Vanderjagt extra point.
	3-yard touchdown pass (Manning to Harrison), Vanderjagt extra point.
4th Quarter:	7-yard touchdown pass (Manning to Stokley), Vanderjagt extra point.

New England

1st Quarter:	32-yard field goal (Vinatieri)
2nd Quarter:	16-yard touchdown pass (Brady to Branch), Vinatieri extra point. 43-yard field goal (Vinatieri)
3rd Quarter:	25-yard touchdown pass (Brady to Patten), Vinatieri extra point. 8-yard touchdown pass (Brady to Graham), Vinatieri extra point.

Game Statistics

	Indianapolis	New England
Total First Downs	28	22
Total Net Yards	446	402
Total Offensive Plays	72	57
Net Yards Rushing	202	82
Net Yards Passing	244	320
Passing		
Attempts-Completions-Inter.	29-16-1	38-26-1
Punts, # - Avg.	2 - 41.0	3 - 47.3
Penalties, # - yards	3-20	8-55
Touchdowns, Total	3	3
Rushing	1	0
Passing	2	3
Field Goals made-attempts	1-2	2-2
Final Score	24	27
Time of Possession	31:41	28:19

Attendance: 68,756
Time: 3:00

Game 2

Indianapolis Colts @
Tennessee Titans
September 19, 2004

Game Summary

The Colts welcomed the Titans after 10 days of needed rest. After losing their opening game of the 2004 season, no one on the team was talking about going 0-2. In this battle of co-MVP quarterbacks from the previous season, it was Peyton Manning who came out on top.

The Colts found themselves in a hole after Tennessee drove 78 yards for a touchdown on their opening drive, with Chris Brown running the ball into the end zone from the 20-yard line. Indianapolis hustled back with a 66-yard drive that was capped by a Mike Vanderjagt 28-yard field goal. COLTS 3, TITANS 7.

After a 58-yard kickoff and an 11-yard return, the Titans marched all the way to the Colts 4-yard line, before turning the ball over after a failed 4th-down attempt. The Colts then turned the ball over on downs, failing to achieve a 1st down on the drive. The Titans took over possession on the Titans 47-yard line and began a 9-play, 32-yard drive that ended with a 39-yard field goal by Gary Anderson. COLTS 3, TITANS 10. Indianapolis returned the kickoff for 18 yards and 5 plays later punted from the Titans 39. Both the Colts and Titans had two more possessions in the 1st half, neither of them covering more than 4 plays. At halftime: COLTS 3, TITANS 10.

The Colts opened the 2nd half primed for a comeback. Peyton Manning moved the Colts toward the end zone, taking advantage of two Titans penalties. Manning capped the 75-yard drive with a 5-yard touchdown pass to Reggie Wayne (**Manning's 3rd of the season**). COLTS 10, TITANS 10.

Don't count the Titans out yet however, as last year's co-MVP Steve McNair moves the Titans 74 yards in 6 plays, running the ball into the end zone from the 1-yard line to score. COLTS 10, TITANS 17.

The Colts then move the ball just 12 yards in 6 plays, resulting in a Hunter Smith punt. The Titans punt after 5 plays, and the Colts finish out the 3rd quarter in impressive fashion, moving the ball 79 yards before Peyton Manning opens the 4th quarter with a touchdown pass to Marcus Pollard from the 1-yard line (**Manning's 4th of the season**). COLTS 17, TITANS 17.

The Titans then drive the ball from their own 40 to the Indianapolis 20 before the Colts intercept a McNair pass. Peyton Manning then utilizes his no-huddle offense to move the ball towards his end zone, finishing with an Edgerrin James 4-yard touchdown run. COLTS 24, TITANS 17. The Titans take the ensuing kickoff and move the ball back to midfield, turning the ball over on downs after a failed fake punt that resulted in a completed pass short of the first down markers.

Peyton Manning then teams with Edgerrin James and Marcus Pollard to move 54 yards in under two minutes, with James marching into the end zone from the 30-yard line. COLTS 31, TITANS 17. The Titans then move the ball from their own 26 to the Colts' 19, ending their drive with a fumble. Peyton Manning closes the game by "taking a knee" on the Titans' 36-yard line.

COLTS 31, TITANS 17 — FINAL

Peyton Manning — 2 touchdown passes

Passing the Record

Dan Marino, Miami Dolphins	1984	Peyton Manning, Indianapolis Colts	2004
Opponent	TD	*Opponent*	TD
Washington	5	New England	2
New England	2	Tennessee	2
Buffalo		Green Bay	
Indianapolis		Jacksonville	
St. Louis		Oakland	
Pittsburgh		Jacksonville	
Houston		Kansas City	
New England		Minnesota	
Buffalo		Houston	
New York		Chicago	
Philadelphia		Detroit	
San Diego		Tennessee	
New York		Houston	
Los Angeles		Baltimore	
Indianapolis		San Diego	
Dallas		Denver	
Through 2 Games	7	**Through 2 Games**	4

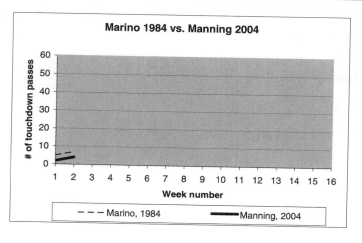

26

Scoring Summary

Box Score

Team ↓ Quarter →	1	2	3	4	Score
Indianapolis	3	0	7	21	31
Tennessee	7	3	7	0	17

Indianapolis

1st Quarter: 28-yard field goal (Vanderjagt)

3rd Quarter: 5-yard touchdown pass (Manning to Wayne), Vanderjagt extra point

4th Quarter: 1-yard touchdown pass (Manning to Pollard), Vanderjagt extra point
4-yard touchdown run (James). Vanderjagt extra point
30-yard touchdown run (James). Vanderjagt extra point

Tennessee

1st Quarter: 20-yard touchdown run (Brown), Anderson extra point

2nd Quarter: 39-yard field goal (Anderson)

3rd Quarter: 1-yard touchdown run (McNair), Anderson extra point

Game Statistics

	Indianapolis	Tennessee
Total First Downs	27	25
Total Net Yards	373	389
Total Offensive Plays	57	73
Net Yards Rushing	129	153
Net Yards Passing	244	236
Passing		
Attempts-Completions-Inter.	33-24-0	40-26-1
Punts, # -Avg.	3-49.0	2-51.0
Penalties, #-yards	2-21	8-71
Touchdowns, Total	4	2
Rushing	2	2
Passing	2	0
Field Goals, made-attempts	1-1	1-1
Final Score	31	17
Time of Possession	25:05	34:55

Attendance: 68,932
Time: 3:12

Game 3

Indianapolis Colts vs. Green Bay Packers September 26, 2004

Game Summary

It's a classic matchup: Peyton Manning vs. Brett Favre. With 9 touchdown passes between them in this game, you couldn't have expected more! The two quarterbacks teamed for over 750 yards, yet the defensive play by the Colts' Nick Harper and Jason David, caused a turnover that resulted in an Edgerrin James touchdown that put the Colts ahead for good.

The Colts opened the game by quickly taking the ball 66 yards in 5 plays and 1:45 to score on a Peyton Manning pass to Reggie Wayne from the 36-yard line (**Manning's 5th of the season**). COLTS 7, PACKERS 0. The Packers stormed right back to score on a Brett Favre pass to Javon Walker, also from the 36-yard line. COLTS 7, PACKERS 7. Peyton Manning then takes the Colts 60 yards in under 2 minutes, completing the very quick drive with a 28-yard touchdown pass to Marvin Harrison (**Manning's 6th of the season**). COLTS 14, PACKERS 7.

Not to be outdone, Favre returns the favor with a 79-yard touchdown strike to Walker, scoring on a single play. COLTS 14, PACKERS 14. Manning then takes the Colts back up the field, completing another quick drive of just 2:32, covering 72 yards, completed with a 34-yard touchdown pass to Brandon Stokley (**Manning's 7th of the season**). COLTS 21, PACKERS 14. The Packers go just 6 plays before punting, having gained just 4 yards on the drive. The COLTS take over on their 6-yard line, ending the quarter 5 plays later. The 2nd quarter starts just as the 1st quarter did, with Peyton Manning again throwing a touchdown pass, this time to Brandon Stokley from the 27-yard line (**Manning's 8th of the season**). COLTS 28, PACKERS 14.

The Packers return with a 38-yard field goal by Ryan Longwell, and the teams exchange possessions before Peyton Manning completes his 5th touchdown pass of the game, this time to James Mungro from the Green Bay 1-yard line (**Manning's 9th of the season**). COLTS 35, PACKERS 17.

The 3rd quarter opens with Brett Favre taking the Packers 65 yards to a touchdown, completing a pass to Walker from the 12-yard line. COLTS 35, PACKERS 24. Each team has a possession and a punt, with the Colts ending the 3rd quarter with the ball. The 4th quarter opens with Manning taking the Colts to the Green Bay 27, and Mike Vanderjagt completing a 45-yard field goal. COLTS 38, PACKERS 24. The Packers come right back with a touchdown pass from Favre to Donald Driver after a 71-yard kickoff return. COLTS 38, PACKERS 31. Each team exchanges possessions twice before the Colts end the scoring with 1:55 remaining the game, with James running into the end zone from the 1-yard line, a possession resulting from a forced fumble created by the Colts' Stephen Davis.

COLTS 45, PACKERS 31 — FINAL

Peyton Manning — 5 touchdown passes

Passing the Record

Dan Marino, Miami Dolphins	1984	Peyton Manning, Indianapolis Colts	2004
Opponent	TD	*Opponent*	TD
Washington	5	New England	2
New England	2	Tennessee	2
Buffalo	3	Green Bay	5
Indianapolis		Jacksonville	
St. Louis		Oakland	
Pittsburgh		Jacksonville	
Houston		Kansas City	
New England		Minnesota	
Buffalo		Houston	
New York		Chicago	
Philadelphia		Detroit	
San Diego		Tennessee	
New York		Houston	
Los Angeles		Baltimore	
Indianapolis		San Diego	
Dallas		Denver	
Through 3 Games	**10**	**Through 3 Games**	**9**

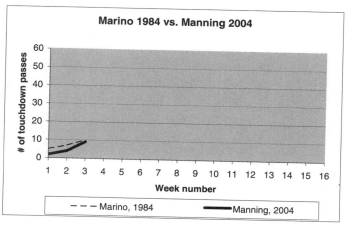

32

Scoring Summary

Box Score

Team ↓ Quarter →	1	2	3	4	Score
Green Bay	14	3	7	7	31
Indianapolis	21	14	0	10	45

Green Bay

1st Quarter: 36-yard touchdown pass (Favre to Walker), Longwell extra point.
79-yard touchdown pass (Favre to Walker), Longwell extra point.

2nd Quarter: 38-yard field goal (Longwell)

3rd Quarter: 12-yard touchdown pass (Favre to Walker), Longwell extra point.

4th Quarter: 27-yard touchdown pass (Favre to Driver), Longwell extra point.

Indianapolis

1st Quarter: 36-yard touchdown pass (Manning to Wayne), Vanderjagt extra point.
28-yard touchdown pass (Manning to Harrison), Vanderjagt extra point
34-yard touchdown pass (Manning to Stokley), Vanderjagt extra point.

2nd Quarter: 27-yard touchdown pass (Manning to Stokley), Vanderjagt extra point
1-yard touchdown pass (Manning to Mungro), Vanderjagt extra point

4th Quarter: 45-yard field goal (Vanderjagt)
1-yard touchdown run (James), Vanderjagt extra point

Game Statistics

	Green Bay	Indianapolis
Total First Downs	24	26
Total Net Yards	459	453
Total Offensive Plays	70	64
Net Yards Rushing	74	60
Net Yards Passing	385	393
Passing		
Attempts-Completions-Inter.	50-34-1	40-28-0
Punts, # -Avg.	4-42.3	4-42.8
Penalties, #-yards	11-84	9-70
Touchdowns, Total	4	6
Rushing	0	1
Passing	4	5
Field Goals, made-attempts	1-2	1-1
Final Score	31	45
Time of Possession	31:08	28:52

Attendance: 57,280
Time: 3:24

Game 4

Indianapolis Colts @ Jacksonville Jaguars October 3, 2004

Game Summary

The Colts came into Jacksonville with a 2-1 record, facing the unbeaten Jaguars. Manning has thrown 9 touchdown passes in the three previous games, just one behind the pace set by Dan Marino in 1984. Manning spread the offense among his teammates, seeing Edgerrin James rack up 83 yards rushing and Brandon Stokley picking up 97 yards receiving.

The Colts opening drive ended with a Hunter Smith punt that gave the Jaguars the ball on their own 28-yard line. Jacksonville advanced to the Colts 24 before turning the ball over after a failed 4th-and-1 play. Manning opened their second drive with a 17-yard strike to Stokley, completed a pass to Harrison and another to Stokley before hitting Marvin Harrison with a 15-yard touchdown pass (**Manning's 10th of the season**). COLTS 7, JAGUARS 0. The rest of the 1st half saw the Colts and Jaguars exchange possessions with the Colts scoring on a 46-yard field goal by Mike Vanderjagt with just under a minute to play in the half. Jacksonville came back with a field goal of their own by Josh Scobee, a 48-yard kick, to end the 1st half. COLTS 10, JAGUARS 3.

The 3rd quarter opened with the Jaguars moving the ball 50-yards toward the end zone, but coming up short, resulting in a Scobee 42-yard field goal. COLTS 10, JAGUARS 6. The Colts and Peyton Manning drove back up the field, covering 83 yards in under 6 minutes, with Marcus Pollard catching a 16-yard touchdown pass from Peyton Manning (**Manning's 11th of the season**). COLTS 17, JAGUARS 6.

After the Vanderjagt kickoff, the Jaguars moved the ball 56 yards, taking them into the 4th quarter, ending the drive with another Scobee field goal. COLTS 17, JAGUARS 9. After an interception of Manning's pass to Dallas Clark, the Jaguars took the ball 49-yards for their first touchdown of the game, a 40-yard touchdown pass from Byron Leftwich to Jimmy Smith and a successful 2-point conversion attempt. COLTS 17, JAGUARS 17.

With 10:32 remaining in the game, the Colts start their possession on their own 26-yard line. A 13-yard drive, evenly mixed with completed passes and a solid running attack, results in a 3-yard touchdown run by Edgerrin James for the final score of the game.

COLTS 24, JAGUARS 17 — FINAL

Peyton Manning — 2 touchdown passes

Passing the Record

Dan Marino, Miami Dolphins	1984	Peyton Manning, Indianapolis Colts	2004
Opponent	TD	*Opponent*	TD
Washington	5	New England	2
New England	2	Tennessee	2
Buffalo	3	Green Bay	5
Indianapolis	2	Jacksonville	2
St. Louis		Oakland	
Pittsburgh		Jacksonville	
Houston		Kansas City	
New England		Minnesota	
Buffalo		Houston	
New York		Chicago	
Philadelphia		Detroit	
San Diego		Tennessee	
New York		Houston	
Los Angeles		Baltimore	
Indianapolis		San Diego	
Dallas		Denver	
Through 4 Games	**12**	**Through 4 Games**	**11**

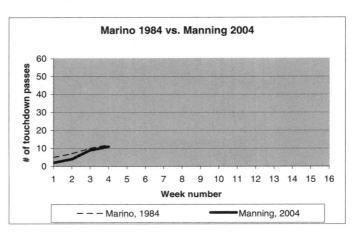

Scoring Summary

Box Score

Team↓Quarter ➔	1	2	3	4	Score
Indianapolis	7	3	7	7	24
Jacksonville	0	3	3	11	17

Indianapolis

1st Quarter:	15-yard touchdown pass (Manning to Harrison), Vanderjagt extra point.
2nd Quarter:	46-yard field goal (Vanderjagt)
3rd Quarter:	16-yard touchdown pass (Manning to Pollard), Vanderjagt extra point.
4th Quarter:	3-yard touchdown run (James), Vanderjagt extra point

Jacksonville

2nd Quarter:	48-yard field goal (Scobee)
3rd Quarter:	42-yard field goal (Scobee)
4th Quarter:	22-yard field goal (Scobee) 40-yard touchdown pass (Leftwich to Smith), 2-point conversion.

Game Statistics

	Indianapolis	Jacksonville
Total First Downs	23	23
Total Net Yards	337	408
Total Offensive Plays	56	73
Net Yards Rushing	117	97
Net Yards Passing	220	311
Passing		
Attempts-Completions-Inter.	29-20-1	41-29-0
Punts, # -Avg.	3-48.0	1-33.0
Penalties, #-yards	3-26	5-28
Touchdowns, Total	3	1
Rushing	1	0
Passing	2	1
Field Goals, made-attempts	1-1	3-4
Final Score	24	17
Time of Possession	24:27	35:33

Attendance: 73,117
Time: 3:09

Game 5

Indianapolis Colts vs. Oakland Raiders October 10, 2004

Game Summary

Back home on their own turf, the Colts were prepared to take care of the Raiders. They did so in convincing fashion, seeing Peyton Manning toss 3 more touchdown passes, and bringing his season total to 14, just one behind Dan Marino's total through five games. This Colts victory marked their 4th straight, and was played without All-Pro kicker Mike Vanderjagt who sat out with a strained right-hamstring. Newly signed Matt Bryant filled the kicking role. This win takes the Colts into their Bye week, a much-needed rest.

Peyton Manning wasted no time with the Raiders, taking the Colts on their first possession, 55 yards in just over 6 minutes, to a touchdown on a 1-yard pass to James Mungro (**Manning's 12th of the season**). COLTS 7, RAIDERS 0. The rest of the 1st quarter saw no scoring with exchanges of possession by both teams. The Colts continued their quarter-ending drive into the 2nd quarter, capped by Peyton Manning's touchdown pass to Reggie Wayne from the 35-yard line (**Manning's 13th of the season**), a 72-yard, 3:05 play drive. COLTS 14, RAIDERS 0.

The Raiders came right back, moving the ball 69 yards in just under 4:30 with a 1-yard touchdown run by Justin Fargas. COLTS 14, RAIDERS 7. Rhodes returns the kickoff 35 yards to give the Colts good field position. A balanced attack by Manning moves the Colts 66 yards in just over 6 minutes, resulting in a Peyton Manning 4-yard touchdown pass to Dallas Clark (**Manning's 14th of the season**) for the last score of the 1st half. COLTS 21, RAIDERS 7.

The 3rd quarter sees no touchdowns nor field goals, as each team moves the ball significantly, but fails to score. The Colts final drive in the 3rd quarter extends into the 4th, resulting in Edgerrin James' 1-yard touchdown run, the result of an 80-yard drive. COLTS 28, RAIDERS 7. After a Colts interception of a Raiders pass and a failed field goal attempt by Matt Bryant, the Raiders move the ball 65 yards resulting in a 21-yard touchdown pass. COLTS 28, RAIDERS 14.

After exchanging 4th quarter possessions, the Colts score for the final time of the game on a Jason David interception of Kerry Collins, which he ran back for a 34-yard touchdown.

COLTS 35, RAIDERS 14 — FINAL

Peyton Manning — 3 touchdown passes

Passing the Record

Dan Marino, Miami Dolphins	1984	Peyton Manning, Indianapolis Colts	2004
Opponent	TD	*Opponent*	TD
Washington	5	New England	2
New England	2	Tennessee	2
Buffalo	3	Green Bay	5
Indianapolis	2	Jacksonville	2
St. Louis	3	Oakland	3
Pittsburgh		Jacksonville	
Houston		Kansas City	
New England		Minnesota	
Buffalo		Houston	
New York		Chicago	
Philadelphia		Detroit	
San Diego		Tennessee	
New York		Houston	
Los Angeles		Baltimore	
Indianapolis		San Diego	
Dallas		Denver	
Through 5 Games	**15**	**Through 5 Games**	**14**

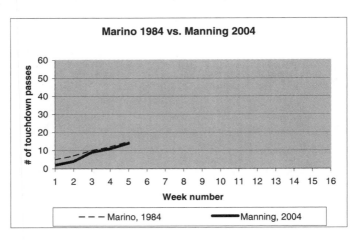

Marino 1984 vs. Manning 2004

- - - Marino, 1984   ━━━Manning, 2004

Scoring Summary

Box Score

Team ↓ Quarter →	1	2	3	4	Score
Oakland	0	7	0	7	14
Indianapolis	7	14	0	14	35

Oakland

2nd Quarter: 1-yard touchdown run (Fargas), Janikowski extra point.

4th Quarter: 21-yard touchdown pass (Collins to Anderson), Janikowski extra point.

Indianapolis

1st Quarter: 1-yard touchdown pass (Manning to Mungro), Bryant extra point.

2nd Quarter: 35-yard touchdown pass (Manning to Wayne), Bryant extra point.
4-yard touchdown pass (Manning to Clark), Bryant extra point.

4th Quarter: 1-yard touchdown run (James), Bryant extra point. 34-yard interception return (David), Bryant extra point.

Game Statistics

	Oakland	Indianapolis
Total First Downs	18	25
Total Net Yards	269	338
Total Offensive Plays	61	67
Net Yards Rushing	53	150
Net Yards Passing	216	188
Passing		
Attempts-Completions-Inter.	44-28-3	26-16-1
Punts, # -Avg.	4-55.5	3-52.0
Penalties, #-yards	9-59	2-20
Touchdowns, Total	2	8
Rushing	1	1
Passing	1	3
Field Goals, made-attempts	0-0	0-1
Final Score	14	35
Time of Possession	24:59	35:01

Attendance: 57,230
Time: 3:05

Indianapolis Colts vs. Jacksonville Jaguars October 24, 2004

Game Summary

The Colts come off their Bye week, well rested, to the stiff competition of the 4-2 Jaguars. Peyton Manning's 3 touchdown passes in this game will bring him even with Dan Marino's total after 6 games, but unfortunately, in a loss for the Colts.

The opening quarter saw both teams move the ball to near or across mid-field, but neither team was able to get near the end zone. The quarter-ending drive by the Jaguars extended into the 2nd quarter, with a 4-yard touchdown pass from Leftwich to Brady. COLTS 0, JAGUARS 7. Peyton Manning and the Colts stormed right back, however, moving the ball 92 yards in just over 4 minutes, ending with a Peyton Manning 7 yard touchdown pass to Marvin Harrison (**Manning's 15th of the season**). COLTS 7, JAGUARS 7.

Jacksonville took the Vanderjagt kickoff and marched towards the end zone, using 7:31 off the clock, covering 62 yards, and resulting in a field goal by Scobee. COLTS 7, JAGUARS 10. Peyton Manning's no-huddle offense advanced the Colts 80 yards in 9 plays with the final score of the 1st half, a Peyton Manning 17-yard touchdown pass to Dallas Clark (**Manning's 16th of the season**). COLTS 14, JAGUARS 10.

The 3rd quarter resulted in only one score — a 32-yard field goal by the Jaguars with 3:11 remaining in the quarter. COLTS 14, JAGUARS 13. After a Colts fumble, the Jaguars took advantage of good field possession, with another field goal by Scobee, this time a 26-yard attempt, taking them into the 4th quarter. COLTS 14, JAGUARS 16. The Colts took over after the Scobee kickoff. A reviewed play nullified a 9-yard touchdown pass from Manning to Harrison, and the Colts settled for a 34-yard field goal by Mike Vanderjagt. COLTS 17, JAGUARS 16.

The Jaguars came back with a 68-yard, 3:18 minute drive with a 25-yard touchdown pass from Leftwitch to Jimmy Smith, and a successful 2-point conversion. The Colts countered with a Peyton Manning 39-yard touchdown strike to Marvin Harrison (**Manning's 17th of the season**). COLTS 24, JAGUARS 24. On the next possession, the Jaguars took the kickoff 27 yards and then moved the ball 30 more yards to set up a 53-yard field goal by Scobee, ending the scoring for the day with 43 seconds remaining in the game.

COLTS 24, JAGUARS 27 — FINAL

Peyton Manning — 3 touchdown passes

Passing the Record

Dan Marino, Miami Dolphins	1984	Peyton Manning, Indianapolis Colts	2004
Opponent	TD	*Opponent*	TD
Washington	5	New England	2
New England	2	Tennessee	2
Buffalo	3	Green Bay	5
Indianapolis	2	Jacksonville	2
St. Louis	3	Oakland	3
Pittsburgh	2	Jacksonville	3
Houston		Kansas City	
New England		Minnesota	
Buffalo		Houston	
New York		Chicago	
Philadelphia		Detroit	
San Diego		Tennessee	
New York		Houston	
Los Angeles		Baltimore	
Indianapolis		San Diego	
Dallas		Denver	
Through 6 Games	**17**	**Through 6 Games**	**17**

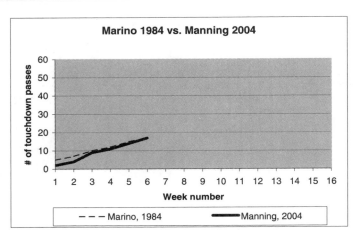

50

Scoring Summary

Box Score

Team ↓ Quarter →	1	2	3	4	Score
Jacksonville	0	10	3	14	27
Indianapolis	0	14	0	10	24

Jacksonville

2nd Quarter: 4-yard touchdown pass (Leftwich to Brady), Scobee extra point.
26-yard field goal (Scobee)

3rd Quarter: 32-yard field goal (Scobee)

4th Quarter: 26-yard field goal (Scobee)
26-yard touchdown pass (Leftwich to Smith), 2-point conversion successful.
53-yard field goal (Scobee)

Indianapolis

2nd Quarter: 7-yard touchdown pass (Manning to Harrison), Vanderjagt extra point.
17-yard touchdown pass (Manning to Clark), Vanderjagt extra point.

4th Quarter: 9-yard touchdown pass (Manning to Harrison), Vanderjagt extra point. (nullified by reviewed play)
34-yard field goal (Vanderjagt)
39-yard touchdown pass (Manning to Harrison), Vanderjagt extra point.

Game Statistics

	Jacksonville	Indianapolis
Total First Downs	20	23
Total Net Yards	414	446
Total Offensive Plays	60	59
Net Yards Rushing	128	87
Net Yards Passing	286	359
Passing		
Attempts-Completions-Inter.	30-23-1	40-27-0
Punts, # -Avg.	1-36.0	3-48.0
Penalties, #-yards	6-48	12-62
Touchdowns, Total	2	3
Rushing	0	0
Passing	2	3
Field Goals, made-attempts	4-4	1-1
Final Score	27	24
Time of Possession	34:34	25:26

Attendance: 56,615
Time: 3:15

Game 7

Indianapolis Colts @ Kansas City Chiefs October 31, 2004

Game Summary

The Colts go into Kansas City after losing their 1ˢᵗ game after 4 consecutive wins. This Halloween game saw 1,095 total yards on offense, Peyton Manning setting a career-best passing mark of 472 yards and four Colts receivers with at least 40 yards. It ended, however, in a Colts defeat.

The Colts open the game and punt just 5 plays later. Fortunately, the Chiefs return the favor by fumbling on the Colts 7 yard line. Manning then takes the Colts 96 yards, capping the drive with a 52-yard touchdown pass to Marvin Harrison (**Manning's 18ᵗʰ of the season**). COLTS 7, CHIEFS 0. The Chiefs come right back, however, scoring in just 6 plays on a 21-yard touchdown pass. COLTS 7, CHIEFS 7.

The 2ⁿᵈ quarter starts with a Chiefs drive that ended the 1ˢᵗ quarter, this 3-play drive came after a 46-yard punt return and ends with a 7-yard touchdown pass. COLTS 7, CHIEFS 14. The Colts return the kickoff 23 yards and end their drive with a Hunter Smith punt. The Chiefs start their drive on their own 17, moving 83 yards in 3:04 to score on a Priest Holmes 21-yard touchdown run. COLTS 7, CHIEFS 21.

The Colts come right back, however, scoring 5 plays later, covering 70 yards. Peyton Manning hits Marcus Pollard with a 5-yard touchdown pass (**Manning's 19ᵗʰ of the season**). COLTS 14, CHIEFS 21. The Chiefs return the kickoff 31 yards, and their 1ˢᵗ pass play covers 52 yards. An 11-yard touchdown run finishes the drive. COLTS 14, CHIEFS 28. The Colts next possession results in a Hunter Smith Punt, and the Chiefs take over on their own 7-yard line. 9 plays and 80 yards later the Chiefs are again on the scoreboard, this time with a 32-yard field goal.

COLTS 14, CHIEFS 31. Mike Vanderjagt attempts a 54-yard field goal and misses, a rarity for Vanderjagt. The Chiefs take over on their own 45-yard line to end the 3rd quarter.

The Chiefs' drive continues in the 4th quarter, but results in a punt. The Colts strike quickly with a 92-yard drive on just 3 plays ending in a Peyton Manning 22-yard touchdown pass to Marvin Harrison (**Manning's 20th of the season**). COLTS 21, CHIEFS 31. The Colts recover the ball after a fumble on a Chiefs field goal attempt, and go 76-yards in 3 plays, to see Reggie Wayne catch a 41-yard touchdown pass from Peyton Manning (**Manning's 21st of the season**). COLTS 28, CHIEFS 31.

The Chiefs' next possession spans from the 3rd quarter into the 4th, and results in a 1-yard touchdown run. COLTS 28, CHIEFS 38. Each team has a possession that ends in a punt, and the Colts again go to the air with Peyton Manning's 5th touchdown pass of the game, hitting Reggie Wayne with a 6-yard touchdown pass (**Manning's 22nd of the season**). COLTS 35, CHIEFS 38. The Chiefs come right back with an 8-play, 70-yard drive and a 14-yard touchdown pass. COLTS 35, CHIEFS 45.

The Colts have one last chance with just over 2 minutes remaining, but a Peyton Manning pass is intercepted at the Chiefs' 25-yard line.

COLTS 35, CHIEFS 45 — FINAL

Peyton Manning — 5 touchdown passes

Passing the Record

Dan Marino, Miami Dolphins	1984	Peyton Manning, Indianapolis Colts	2004
Opponent	TD	*Opponent*	TD
Washington	5	New England	2
New England	2	Tennessee	2
Buffalo	3	Green Bay	5
Indianapolis	2	Jacksonville	2
St. Louis	3	Oakland	3
Pittsburgh	2	Jacksonville	3
Houston	3	Kansas City	5
New England		Minnesota	
Buffalo		Houston	
New York		Chicago	
Philadelphia		Detroit	
San Diego		Tennessee	
New York		Houston	
Los Angeles		Baltimore	
Indianapolis		San Diego	
Dallas		Denver	
Through 7 Games	**20**	**Through 7 Games**	**22**

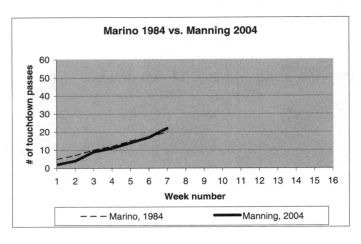

56

Scoring Summary

Box Score

Team ↓ Quarter →	1	2	3	4	Score
Indianapolis	7	7	14	7	35
Kansas City	7	24	0	14	45

Indianapolis

1st Quarter: 52-yard touchdown pass (Manning to Harrison), Vanderjagt extra point.

2nd Quarter: 5-yard touchdown pass (Manning to Pollard), Vanderjagt extra point.

3rd Quarter: 22-yard touchdown pass (Manning to Harrison), Vanderjagt extra point. 41-yard touchdown pass (Manning to Wayne), Vanderjagt extra point.

4th Quarter: 6-yard touchdown pass (Manning to Wayne), Vanderjagt extra point.

Kansas City

1st Quarter: 21-yard touchdown pass (Green to Gonzalez), Tynes extra point.

2nd Quarter: 7-yard touchdown pass (Green to Morton), Tynes extra point. 21-yard touchdown run (Holmes), Tynes extra point. 11-yard touchdown run Holmes), Tynes extra point. 32-yard field goal (Tynes)

4th Quarter: 1-yard touchdown run (Holmes), Tynes extra point. 14-yard touchdown pass (Green to Gonzalez), Tynes extra point.

Game Statistics

	Indianapolis	Kansas City
Total First Downs	23	33
Total Net Yards	505	590
Total Offensive Plays	56	77
Net Yards Rushing	33	203
Net Yards Passing	472	387
Passing		
Attempts-Completions-Inter.	44-25-1	34-27-0
Punts, # -Avg.	4-44.5	2-38.5
Penalties, #-yards	7-40	5-46
Touchdowns, Total	5	6
Rushing	0	3
Passing	5	3
Field Goals, made-attempts	0-1	1-1
Final Score	35	45
Time of Possession	22:27	37:33

Attendance: 78,312
Time: 3:25

Game 8

Indianapolis Colts vs. Minnesota Vikings November 8, 2004

Game Summary

The Colts have lost two in a row. Peyton Manning is ahead of Dan Marino's record-setting pace by 2 coming into the game, and it's MONDAY NIGHT! In this prime-time matchup, it's Manning's passing that keeps the Colts in the game, and Mike Vanderjagt's leg that secures the victory.

The Vikings opened the game going "4 and out" and promptly punted. The Colts took over on their own 49-yard line, and sent the ball with Edgerrin James on 5 consecutive plays. Manning ended the drive with a 5-yard touchdown pass to Reggie Wayne (**Manning's 23rd of the year**), capping a 51-yard drive. COLTS 7, VIKINGS 0. The next Vikings drive again results in a punt, giving the Colts the ball on their own 22-yard line. 11 plays later, and just into the 2nd quarter, Peyton Manning hits Marcus Pollard with a 10-yard touchdown pass (**Manning's 24th of the year**). COLTS 14, VIKINGS 0.

The Vikings storm back after a 51-yard kickoff return and score 4 plays later on a Morten Andersen field goal from the 24-yard line. COLTS 14, VIKINGS 3. After a 14-play drive that ended in a Hunter Smith punt, the Vikings take over on their own 8-yard line, and end the 2nd quarter with another Andersen field goal, this time from the 5-yard line. COLTS 14, VIKINGS 6.

The 3rd quarter starts with a Colts drive that results in a Hunter Smith punt that is returned 91 yards for a touchdown. The Vikings successfully convert the 2-point conversion. COLTS 14, VIKINGS 14. Both teams have a possession and punt, with the Colts then moving the ball 87 yards in 7 plays to complete the scoring in the 3rd quarter on a Peyton Manning touchdown pass to Dallas Clark from the 4-yard line (**Manning's 25th of the year**). COLTS 21, VIKINGS 14.

The 4th quarter opens with the Vikings continuing a drive from the end of Quarter 3. This play results in a touchdown pass from Daunte Culpepper to Nate Burleson from the 8-yard line. COLTS 21, VIKINGS 21. The Colts come right back, scoring in just 7 plays after the kickoff is returned for 44 yards. Manning hits Marcus Pollard for a 19-yard touchdown pass (**Manning's 26th of the season**). COLTS 28, VIKINGS 21. The Vikings come back with a 7 play, 65-yard drive resulting in a 24-yard touchdown run by Smith. COLTS 28, VIKINGS 28.

With under 3 minutes left in the game, Peyton Manning moves the Colts to the Vikings' 18-yard line, providing Mike Vanderjagt the opportunity to win the game with a 35-yard field goal, the 10th game-winning field goal in his career.

COLTS 31, VIKINGS 28 — FINAL

Peyton Manning — 4 touchdown passes

Passing the Record

Dan Marino, Miami Dolphins	1984	Peyton Manning, Indianapolis Colts	2004
Opponent	TD	*Opponent*	TD
Washington	5	New England	2
New England	2	Tennessee	2
Buffalo	3	Green Bay	5
Indianapolis	2	Jacksonville	2
St. Louis	3	Oakland	3
Pittsburgh	2	Jacksonville	3
Houston	3	Kansas City	5
New England	4	Minnesota	4
Buffalo		Houston	
New York		Chicago	
Philadelphia		Detroit	
San Diego		Tennessee	
New York		Houston	
Los Angeles		Baltimore	
Indianapolis		San Diego	
Dallas		Denver	
Through 8 Games	24	**Through 8 Games**	26

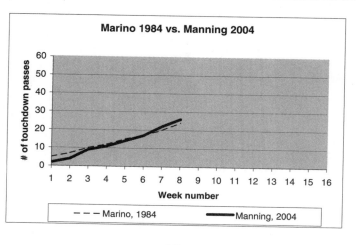

62

Scoring Summary

Box Score

Team ↓ Quarter →	1	2	3	4	Score
Minnesota	0	6	8	14	28
Indianapolis	7	7	7	10	31

Minnesota

2nd Quarter: 42-yard field goal (Andersen)
23-yard field goal (Andersen)

3rd Quarter: 91-yard punt return (Burleson) 2 point conversion (Culpepper)

4th Quarter: 8-yard touchdown pass (Culpepper to Burleson)
24-yard touchdown run (Smith)

Indianapolis

1st Quarter: 5-yard touchdown pass (Manning to Wayne), Vanderjagt extra point.

2nd Quarter: 10-yard touchdown pass (Manning to Pollard), Vanderjagt extra point.

3rd Quarter: 4-yard touchdown pass (Manning to Clark), Vanderjagt extra point.

4th Quarter: 19-yard touchdown pass (Manning to Pollard), Vanderjagt extra point.
35-yard field goal (Vanderjagt)

Game Statistics

	Minnesota	Indianapolis
Total First Downs	15	26
Total Net Yards	292	408
Total Offensive Plays	45	61
Net Yards Rushing	138	144
Net Yards Passing	154	264
Passing		
Attempts-Completions-Inter.	19-16-0	29-23-0
Punts, # -Avg.	3-36.7	3-41.0
Penalties, #-yards	6-53	8-65
Touchdowns, Total	3	4
Rushing	1	0
Passing	1	4
Field Goals, made-attempts	2-2	1-1
Final Score	28	31
Time of Possession	25:48	34:12

Attendance: 57,307
Time: 3:02

Indianapolis Colts quarterback Peyton Manning (18) hands off to running back Edgerrin James against the Oakland Raiders, Sunday, Oct. 10, 2004, in Indianapolis. Manning completed 16 of 26 passes for 198 yards and three touchdowns, while James ran for 136 yards and a score to lead the Colts past the Raiders, 35-14, for their fourth straight win. (AP/Wide World Photos)

Indianapolis Colts quarterback Peyton Manning throws a pass against the Minnesota Vikings during the fourth quarter in Indianapolis, Monday, Nov.8, 2004. The Colts won 31-28. Manning had 268 yards passing and four touchdowns. (AP/Wide World Photos)

Indianapolis Colts quarterback Peyton Manning throws a 12-yard touchdown pass against the Houston Texans during the first quarter Sunday, Dec. 12, 2004, in Houston. (AP/Wide World Photos)

Indianapolis Colts quarterback Peyton Manning, left, makes a second-quarter pass despite defensive pressure from Jacksonville Jaguars' Tommy Hendricks, right, Sunday, Oct. 3, 2004, in Jacksonville, Fla. (AP/Wide World Photos)

Indianapolis Colts quarterback Peyton Manning throws his 49th touchdown pass of the season to Brandon Stokley during the fourth quarter against the San Diego Chargers in Indianapolis, Sunday, Dec. 26, 2004. The Colts won 34-31 in overtime. The pass broke Dan Marino's record. (AP/Wide World Photos)

Indianapolis Colts quarterback Peyton Manning reacts after the Colts scored on a two-point conversion to tie the game at 31 against the San Diego Chargers in Indianapolis, Sunday, Dec. 26, 2004. The Colts won in overtime 34-31. (AP/Wide World Photos)

Indianapolis Colts quarterback Peyton Manning raises his fist after throwing his 49th touchdown pass during the fourth quarter against the San Diego Chargers in Indianapolis, Sunday, Dec. 26, 2004. The Colts won in overtime, 34-31. Manning broke Dan Marino's record for number of touchdown passes in a single season. (AP/Wide World Photos)

Indianapolis Colts Peyton Manning (18) throws a pass in the third quarter during the AFC wild-card game against the Denver Broncos in Indianapolis, Sunday, Jan. 9, 2005. The Colts won 49-24. (AP/Wide World Photos)

Indianapolis Colts quarterback Peyton Manning points to the crowd near the end of the AFC wild-card game against the Denver Broncos in Indianapolis, Sunday, Jan. 9, 2005. The Colts defeated the Broncos 49-24 and will face the New England Patriots next Sunday. Manning threw for 457 yards, and 4 touchdowns, and scored a touchdown on a run. (AP/Wide World Photos)

Game 9

Indianapolis Colts vs.
Houston Texans
November 14, 2004

Game Summary

Peyton Manning is now 4 touchdown passes ahead of the pace set by Dan Marino in 1984. This game is another 5-touchdown game, and the excitement is starting to grow around Peyton Manning and the Indianapolis Colts.

The Texans opened the game with the ball and punted after 4 plays. The Colts moved the ball 65-yards in 11 plays, with Peyton Manning throwing a 4-yard touchdown pass to Brandon Stokley (**Manning's 27th of the season**). COLTS 7, TEXANS 0. The Texans punt, followed by a Colts punt and another Texans punt. The Colts end the 1st quarter with the ball and continue that possession in the 2nd quarter.

The Colts continue their possession by moving the ball 69 yards in 10 plays, ending the drive with another Peyton Manning touchdown pass, this time to Reggie Wayne (**Manning's 28th of the season**). COLTS 14, TEXANS 0. After a failed field goal attempt by the Texans, the Colts take over on their 45, but the drive results in a Hunter Smith punt. The Texans punt on their next possession as well, and the Colts make short work of the drive, going 29 yards in 2 plays, after a 34-yard return on a 15-yard punt. Peyton Manning connects with Dallas Clark for a 1-yard touchdown pass (**Manning's 29th of the season**) to end the scoring in the 1st half. COLTS 21, TEXANS 0.

The 2nd half opens with the Colts returning the kickoff 29 yards, a 3-yard run from scrimmage by Edgerrin James, and a Peyton Manning 69-yard touchdown pass to Brandon Stokley (**Manning's 30th of the season**). COLTS 28, TEXANS 0. The Texans' quarterback is sacked on the 3rd play of their next drive, resulting in a Colts touchdown on a

37-yard fumble recovery by Bob Sanders. COLTS 35, TEXANS 0. The Texans move the ball all the way to the Colts 6-yard line before throwing an interception. 3 plays later, a Peyton Manning pass intended for Brandon Stokley is intercepted at the Indianapolis 30-yard line. The Texans then go 16 yards in 7 plays for their first score of the game, a 1-yard touchdown run. COLTS 35, TEXANS 7.

The Colts finish the 3rd quarter with a 65-yard drive, using just 2 plays and less than a minute off the clock. Peyton Manning tosses his 5th touchdown pass of the game to Dallas Clark from the Indianapolis 20, an 80-yard touchdown pass (**Manning's 31st of the season**). COLTS 42, TEXANS 7.

The 4th quarter opens with an exchange of possessions and the Texans scoring on a 1-yard touchdown run with 7:50 remaining in the game. COLTS 42, TEXANS 7. The Colts next possession results in a Hunter Smith punt. The Colts' Von Hutchins then intercepts a Texans pass on the Colts' 23, returning it 77 yards for a touchdown.

COLTS 49, TEXANS 14 — FINAL

Peyton Manning — 5 touchdown passes

Passing the Record

Dan Marino, Miami Dolphins	1984	Peyton Manning, Indianapolis Colts	2004
Opponent	TD	*Opponent*	TD
Washington	5	New England	2
New England	2	Tennessee	2
Buffalo	3	Green Bay	5
Indianapolis	2	Jacksonville	2
St. Louis	3	Oakland	3
Pittsburgh	2	Jacksonville	3
Houston	3	Kansas City	5
New England	4	Minnesota	4
Buffalo	3	Houston	5
New York		Chicago	
Philadelphia		Detroit	
San Diego		Tennessee	
New York		Houston	
Los Angeles		Baltimore	
Indianapolis		San Diego	
Dallas		Denver	
Through 9 Games	**27**	**Through 9 Games**	**31**

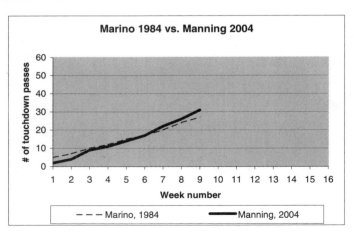

Scoring Summary

Box Score

Team ↓ Quarter →	1	2	3	4	Score
Houston	0	0	7	7	14
Indianapolis	7	14	21	7	49

Houston

3rd Quarter: 1-yard touchdown run (Davis), Brown extra point.

4th Quarter: 1-yard touchdown run (Davis), Brown extra point.

Indianapolis

1st Quarter: 4-yard touchdown pass (Manning to Stokley), Vanderjagt extra point.

2nd Quarter: 5-yard touchdown pass (Manning to Wayne), Vanderjagt extra point.
1-yard touchdown pass (Manning to Clark), Vanderjagt extra point.

3rd Quarter: 69-yard touchdown pass (Manning to Stokley), Vanderjagt extra point.
37-yard fumble return (Sanders), Vanderjagt extra point.
80-yard touchdown pass (Manning to Clark), Vanderjagt extra point.

4th Quarter: 77-yard interception return (Hutchins), Vanderjagt extra point.

Game Statistics

	Houston	Indianapolis
Total First Downs	20	17
Total Net Yards	302	398
Total Offensive Plays	83	48
Net Yards Rushing	132	86
Net Yards Passing	170	312
Passing		
Attempts-Completions-Inter.	41-22-3	27-18-2
Punts, # -Avg.	4-33.8	3-41.0
Penalties, #-yards	8-65	11-85
Touchdowns, Total	2	7
Rushing	2	0
Passing	0	5
Field Goals, made-attempts	0-1	0-1
Final Score	14	49
Time of Possession	35:41	21:19

Attendance: 56,511
Time: 3:29

Game 10

Indianapolis Colts @ Chicago Bears November 21, 2004

Game Summary

The "Monsters of the Midway" were given a dose of Colts' Pride at Soldier Field. Edgerrin James ran for 204 yards on 23 carries while Peyton Manning struck for 4 touchdown passes on the day. Both superstars took an early rest, enjoying the game from the sidelines during the 4th quarter.

Chicago's opening possession resulted in a 33-yard punt, giving the Colts the ball on their own 27-yard line. Peyton Manning kick-starts the Colts' offense with a "no huddle" drive that covered 73 yards in 10 plays, capped off with a Manning touchdown pass to Marcus Pollard from the 14-yard line (**Manning's 32nd of the season**). COLTS 7, BEARS 0. The next Bears drive again ends with a punt, but the Colts return the favor, making no forward progress. Hunter Smith punts, giving Chicago the ball on its own 27-yard line. The Bears move the ball 39 yards in 7 plays, resulting in a 51-yard field goal by Paul Edinger. COLTS 7, BEARS 3.

After a 54-yard kick off and 14-yard return, the Colts progress up the field taking the drive into the 2nd quarter, ending in a 35-yard Manning touchdown pass to Reggie Wayne (**Manning's 33rd of the season**). COLTS 14, BEARS 3. Chicago turns the ball over to the Colts on their next possession, via a fumble on their own 29-yard line. The Colts take over and score with a Mike Vanderjagt 34-yard field goal just 2 minutes later. COLTS 17, BEARS 3.

After a Bears punt, a Colts punt, and then a Bears' fumble, Peyton Manning strikes again with a 10-yard touchdown pass to Marvin Harrison (**Manning's 34th of the season**). COLTS 24, BEARS 3. After the Colts' interception of a Bears pass, the Colts move back toward the end zone, using just over 3 minutes to complete the scoring drive with a Vanderjagt 20-yard field goal for the final score of the 1st half. COLTS 27, BEARS 3

The Colts open the 2nd half with a drive that is cut short by a rare Peyton Manning interception. The Bears can't take advantage, however, and have to punt. The Colts take over on their own 29-yard line, and 4 plays later, Manning hits Reggie Wayne with a 27-yard touchdown pass (**Manning's 35th of the season**). COLTS 34, BEARS 3. The Bears mount a charge, moving the ball to the Colts' 34-yard line before a fumble resulting in the Colts gaining possession of the ball. 54 yards and just 7 plays later, Edgerrin James scores on an 11-yard touchdown run. COLTS 43, BEARS 3.

The Bears promptly move toward the end zone, only to have a touchdown pass nullified by an offensive holding penalty. The Colts intercept the next pass in the end zone and take over at the 20-yard line. After a lengthy drive that eats up almost 8 minutes of the quarter, they turn the ball over on downs. Chicago takes advantage, scoring on a 2-yard touchdown pass from rookie Craig Krenzel.

COLTS 43, BEARS 10 — FINAL.

Peyton Manning — 4 touchdown passes

Passing the Record

Dan Marino, Miami Dolphins	1984	Peyton Manning, Indianapolis Colts	2004
Opponent	TD	*Opponent*	TD
Washington	5	New England	2
New England	2	Tennessee	2
Buffalo	3	Green Bay	5
Indianapolis	2	Jacksonville	2
St. Louis	3	Oakland	3
Pittsburgh	2	Jacksonville	3
Houston	3	Kansas City	5
New England	4	Minnesota	4
Buffalo	3	Houston	5
New York	2	Chicago	4
Philadelphia		Detroit	
San Diego		Tennessee	
New York		Houston	
Los Angeles		Baltimore	
Indianapolis		San Diego	
Dallas		Denver	
Through 10 Games	**29**	**Through 10 Games**	**35**

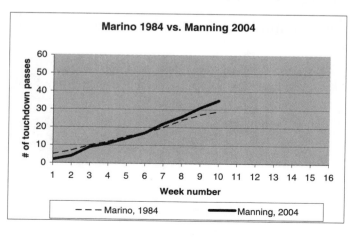

74

Scoring Summary

Box Score

Team ↓ Quarter →	1	2	3	4	Score
Indianapolis	7	20	14	0	41
Chicago	3	0	0	7	10

Indianapolis

1st Quarter: 14-yard touchdown pass (Manning to Pollard), Vanderjagt extra point.

2nd Quarter: 35-yard touchdown pass (Manning to Wayne), Vanderjagt extra point.
34-yard field goal (Vanderjagt)
10-yard touchdown pass (Manning to Harrison), Vanderjagt extra point.
20-yard field goal (Vanderjagt)

3rd Quarter: 27-yard touchdown pass (Manning to Wayne), Vanderjagt extra point.
11-yard touchdown run (James), Vanderjagt extra point.

Chicago

1st Quarter: 51-yard field goal (Edinger)

4th Quarter: 2-yard touchdown pass (Krenzel to Lyman), Edinger extra point.

Game Statistics

	Indianapolis	Chicago
Total First Downs	31	14
Total Net Yards	486	224
Total Offensive Plays	67	54
Net Yards Rushing	275	79
Net Yards Passing	211	145
Passing		
Attempts-Completions-Inter.	28-17-1	24-14-2
Punts, #-Avg.	2-35.0	4-40.8
Penalties, #-yards	10-91	9-50
Touchdowns, Total	5	1
Rushing	1	0
Passing	4	1
Field Goals, made-attempts	2-2	1-1
Final Score	41	10
Time of Possession	35:37	24:23

Attendance: 61,908
Time: 2:58

Game 11

Indianapolis Colts @ Detroit Lions

November 25, 2004

Game Summary

Thanksgiving Day, in front of a national TV audience; Peyton Manning is in Detroit to enjoy his Thanksgiving this year, putting on a clinic about how to manage the offense from the line of scrimmage. The Colts serve up the Lions in a 41-10 romp featuring 6 touchdown passes from Peyton Manning.

The Colts open the game with the ball on their own 21-yard line, and move 79 yards in 9 plays. Manning hits Brandon Stokley with a 4-yard touchdown pass to end the drive (**Manning's 36th of the season**). The Lions come back, taking their drive all the way to the 2-yard line, before having to settle for a field goal. COLTS 7, LIONS 3. Manning takes the Colts back up the field, covering 60 yards in 7 plays and less than 3 minutes, again hitting Brandon Stokley, this time with a 12-yard touchdown pass (**Manning's 37th of the season**). Vanderjagt's extra point attempt is blocked. COLTS 13, LIONS 3.

Detroit marches back up the field after starting at their own 29-yard line, again on the shoulders of their kicker Jason Hanson, who scores with a 34-yard field goal. COLTS 13, LIONS 6. Both teams come up dry for most of the 2nd quarter, until Manning hits Stokley yet again, this time from the 25-yard line with his 3rd touchdown pass of the day (**Manning's 38th of the season**). COLTS 20, LIONS 6. Detroit promptly fumbles on their next possession, setting up a Peyton Manning touchdown pass to Marvin Harrison from the 13-yard line (**Manning's 39th of the season**). The Lions end the 2nd quarter on a 32-yard field goal by Jason Hanson. COLTS 27, LIONS 9.

The Lions open the 2nd half with the ball, but have to punt without seeing a first down. The Colts move back up the field,

64 yards and 8 plays, ending the drive with a Manning 10-yard touchdown pass to Harrison (**Manning's 40th of the season**). COLTS 34, LIONS 9. The Lions again have trouble with the Colts defense, moving the ball just 3 yards before having to punt. The Colts take over on their own 36-yard line, and waste no time in heading for the end zone. Peyton Manning connects on multiple passes, mixed with Edgerrin James runs, ending in Manning's 6th touchdown pass of the day, a 5-yard strike to Marvin Harrison (**Manning's 41st of the season**). COLTS 41, LIONS 9.

The 4th quarter sees both teams with the ball, and Peyton Manning watching from the sideline. Neither team scores in the quarter.

COLTS 41, LIONS 9 — FINAL.

Peyton Manning — 6 touchdown passes

Passing the Record

Dan Marino, Miami Dolphins	1984	Peyton Manning, Indianapolis Colts	2004
Opponent	TD	*Opponent*	TD
Washington	5	New England	2
New England	2	Tennessee	2
Buffalo	3	Green Bay	5
Indianapolis	2	Jacksonville	2
St. Louis	3	Oakland	3
Pittsburgh	2	Jacksonville	3
Houston	3	Kansas City	5
New England	4	Minnesota	4
Buffalo	3	Houston	5
New York	2	Chicago	4
Philadelphia	1	Detroit	6
San Diego		Tennessee	
New York		Houston	
Los Angeles		Baltimore	
Indianapolis		San Diego	
Dallas		Denver	
Through 11 Games	**30**	**Through 11 Games**	**41**

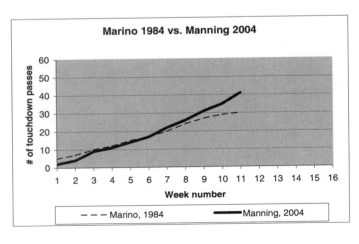

80

Scoring Summary

Box Score

Team ↓ Quarter →	1	2	3	4	Score
Indianapolis	13	14	14	0	41
Detroit	6	3	0	0	9

Indianapolis

1st Quarter: 4-yard touchdown pass (Manning to Stokley), Vanderjagt extra point.
12-yard touchdown pass (Manning to Stokley), Vanderjagt kick blocked.

2nd Quarter: 25-yard touchdown pass (Manning to Stokley), Vanderjagt extra point.
13-yard touchdown pass (Manning to Harrison), Vanderjagt extra point.

3rd Quarter: 10-yard touchdown pass (Manning to Harrison), Vanderjagt extra point.
5-yard touchdown pass (Manning to Harrison), Vanderjagt extra point.

Detroit

1st Quarter: 20-yard field goal (Hanson)
34-yard field goal (Hanson)

2nd Quarter: 32-yard field goal (Hanson)

Game Statistics

	Indianapolis	Detroit
Total First Downs	24	19
Total Net Yards	356	386
Total Offensive Plays	60	62
Net Yards Rushing	113	168
Net Yards Passing	243	218
Passing		
Attempts-Completions-Inter.	31-24-0	38-25-1
Punts, # -Avg.	5-41.8	3-41.0
Penalties, #-yards	5-40	10-60
Touchdowns, Total	6	0
Rushing	0	0
Passing	6	0
Field Goals, made-attempts	0-0	3-4
Final Score	41	9
Time of Possession	31:12	28:48

Attendance: 63,107
Time: 3:14

Game 12

Indianapolis Colts vs.
Tennessee Titans
December 5, 2004

I was
at this
game

Game Summary

The Titans knew they didn't have what they needed against the Colts, so they brought their bag of tricks. Trying everything from on-side kicks to trick plays, the Titans made the 1st quarter interesting.

Peyton Manning made the rest of the game interesting, passing for over 400 yards and helping the Colts put 51 points on the board, while extending his streak of 4-touchdown games to four and tying Johnny Unitas' 45-year old record by throwing multiple touchdown passes in the first 12 games of the season.

The Titans open the game with the ball, but go "4-and-out" giving the Colts the ball on their own 33-yard line after a 40-yard punt. The Colts move to the Titans' 30-yard line and settle for a Mike Vanderjagt 47-yard field goal. The Titans storm back, scoring on their 2nd play, a 48-yard touchdown from Billy Volek to Drew Bennett. The Titans recover the onside kick at their own 47-yard line, and convert the drive into 3 points after a Gary Anderson 45-yard field goal. COLTS 3, TITANS 10

The Titans attempt another onside kick, but the ball goes out-of-bounds and a penalty is issued for a "short free kick." The Titans kick off again, this time sending the ball 63 yards, and the Colts start their drive on their own 34-yard line. Manning moves the Colts up the field in short order, using less than 3 minutes to cover 66 yards. Manning connects with Marvin Harrison for a 24-yard touchdown pass (**Manning's 42nd of the season**). The Titans challenge the play, but the ruling on the field stands. Volek moves the Titans quickly toward the end zone, covering 64 yards in 3 plays to score on a 28-yard touchdown pass to Drew Bennett. COLTS 10, TITANS 17.

After another on-side kick, recovered by the Titans, the Colts intercept a Volek pass at midfield. After a 59-yard pass to Marvin Harrison, Edgerrin James takes the ball over the middle for a 4-yard touchdown run. After a 26-yard kickoff return, the Titans quickly move the ball as the 1st quarter comes to a close, scoring on a Volek 48-yard touchdown pass to Bennett. COLTS 17, TITANS 24.

The 2nd quarter opens with a 87-yard drive, peppered with runs by James and Manning passing out of the shotgun formation. The drive is complete with a 28-yard touchdown pass from Manning to Brandon Stokley (**Manning's 43rd of the season**). The Titans move the ball back to the Colts' 25-yard line and attempt a field goal, which is blocked and recovered by Rob Morris, who returns the ball 68 yards for a touchdown to end the scoring in the 1st half. COLTS 31, TITANS 24.

The 3rd quarter sees the Colts with the ball and a 74-yard drive that ends with a 20-yard field goal by Vanderjagt. The Titans turn the ball over after a failed 4th and 7 attempt and 3 plays later, Edgerrin James scores on a 12-yard touchdown run. COLTS 41, TITANS 24.

The 4th quarter sees the continuation of a Colts drive that started at the end of the 3rd quarter. Manning throws his 3rd touchdown of the day, this time a 10-yard strike to Reggie Wayne (**Manning's 44th of the season**). After a Titan failed drive and a punt, the Colts move the ball 52 yards to end the day's scoring with a Vanderjagt 37-yard field goal.

COLTS 51, TITANS 24 — FINAL.

Peyton Manning — 3 touchdown passes

Passing the Record

Dan Marino, Miami Dolphins	1984	Peyton Manning, Indianapolis Colts	2004
Opponent	TD	*Opponent*	TD
Washington	5	New England	2
New England	2	Tennessee	2
Buffalo	3	Green Bay	5
Indianapolis	2	Jacksonville	2
St. Louis	3	Oakland	3
Pittsburgh	2	Jacksonville	3
Houston	3	Kansas City	5
New England	4	Minnesota	4
Buffalo	3	Houston	5
New York	2	Chicago	4
Philadelphia	1	Detroit	6
San Diego	3	Tennessee	3
New York		Houston	
Los Angeles		Baltimore	
Indianapolis		San Diego	
Dallas		Denver	
Through 12 Games	**32**	**Through 12 Games**	**44**

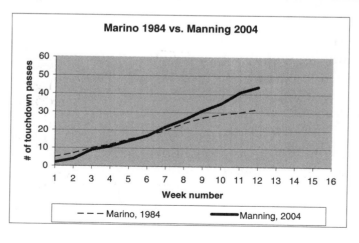

Marino 1984 vs. Manning 2004

86

Scoring Summary

Box Score

Team ↓ Quarter →	1	2	3	4	Score
Tennessee	24	0	0	0	24
Indianapolis	17	14	10	10	51

Tennessee

1st Quarter: 48-yard touchdown pass (Volek to Bennett), Anderson extra point.
45-yard field goal (Anderson)
28-yard touchdown pass (Volek to Bennett), Anderson extra point.
48-yard touchdown pass (Volek to Bennett), Anderson extra point.

Indianapolis

1st Quarter: 47-yard field goal (Vanderjagt)
24-yard touchdown pass (Manning to Harrison), Vanderjagt extra point.
4-yard touchdown run (James), Vanderjagt extra point.

2nd Quarter: 28-yard touchdown pass (Manning to Stokley), Vanderjagt extra point.
68-yard touchdown blocked field goal return (Morris), Vanderjagt extra point.

3rd Quarter: 20-yard field goal (Vanderjagt)
12-yard touchdown run (James), Vanderjagt extra point.

4th Quarter: 10-yard touchdown pass (Manning to Wayne), Vanderjagt extra point.
37-yard field goal (Vanderjagt)

Game Statistics

	Tennessee	Indianapolis
Total First Downs	17	29
Total Net Yards	340	567
Total Offensive Plays	68	63
Net Yards Rushing	115	150
Net Yards Passing	225	417
Passing		
Attempts-Completions-Inter.	36-21-2	34-25-2
Punts, # -Avg.	4-47.3	0-00.0
Penalties, #-yards	9-105	7-88
Touchdowns, Total	3	6
Rushing	0	2
Passing	3	3
Field Goals, made-attempts	1-2	3-3
Final Score	24	51
Time of Possession	33:05	26:55

Attendance: 57,278
Time: 3:24

Game 13

Indianapolis Colts @ Houston Texans December 12, 2004

Game Summary

Peyton Manning goes into Houston aiming to clinch the AFC South Championship with a win. The day proves fruitful, and Manning set another record with his 13th straight multi-touchdown game. In the end, the Colts scored just 23 points, but wrapped up a playoff berth and the AFC South Championship.

The Texans opened the game with the ball, but turned the ball over on their 3rd play after an interception on their own 28-yard line. Manning and the Colts wasted no time, driving 37 yards in 7 plays, scoring on a Manning 3-yard touchdown pass to Marvin Harrison (**Manning's 45th of the season**). The Texans are forced to punt on their next possession, giving the Colts the ball on their own 28-yard line. Manning moves his offense back up the field, covering 72-yards in just 8 plays and less than 5 minutes. The Colts score when Manning connects with Reggie Wayne for a 12-yard touchdown pass (**Manning's 46th of the season**). COLTS 14, TEXANS 0.

In the 2nd quarter, the Texans complete a 42-yard drive and the Colts have to punt. David Carr hits Jonathan Wells with a 3-yard touchdown pass. Each team has another chance to score in the quarter, but neither does. The 1st half comes to a close. COLTS 14, TEXANS 7.

The Colts open the 3rd quarter with the ball and move to the Houston 12-yard line, before scoring on a Mike Vanderjagt 30-yard field goal. The Texans come right back, scoring in just over 5 minutes, covering 74 yards in 9 plays on a

Domanick Davis 15-yard touchdown run. After exchanging possessions to complete the 3rd quarter and start the 4th, the Colts add to their lead with a Vanderjagt 43-yard field goal. COLTS 20, TEXANS 14.

The Texans punt without seeing a first down on their next possession, and the Colts move the ball 49 yards to see Vanderjagt put another 3 points on the scoreboard with his 3rd field goal of the day, this time from 44 yards out, to finish the scoring for the game.

COLTS 23, TEXANS 14 — FINAL.

Peyton Manning — 2 touchdown passes

Passing the Record

Dan Marino, Miami Dolphins	1984	Peyton Manning, Indianapolis Colts	2004
Opponent	TD	*Opponent*	TD
Washington	5	New England	2
New England	2	Tennessee	2
Buffalo	3	Green Bay	5
Indianapolis	2	Jacksonville	2
St. Louis	3	Oakland	3
Pittsburgh	2	Jacksonville	3
Houston	3	Kansas City	5
New England	4	Minnesota	4
Buffalo	3	Houston	5
New York	2	Chicago	4
Philadelphia	1	Detroit	6
San Diego	3	Tennessee	3
New York	4	Houston	2
Los Angeles		Baltimore	
Indianapolis		San Diego	
Dallas		Denver	
Through 13 Games	**36**	**Through 13 Games**	**46**

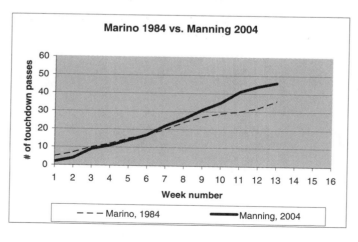

92

Scoring Summary

Box Score

Team ↓ Quarter →	1	2	3	4	Score
Indianapolis	14	0	3	6	23
Houston	0	7	7	0	14

Indianapolis

1st Quarter: 3-yard touchdown pass (Manning to Harrison), Vanderjagt extra point.
12-yard touchdown pass (Manning to Wayne), Vanderjagt extra point.
3rd Quarter: 30-yard field goal (Vanderjagt)
4th Quarter: 43-yard field goal (Vanderjagt)
44-yard field goal (Vanderjagt)

Houston

2nd Quarter: 3-yard touchdown pass (Carr to Wells), Brown extra point.
3rd Quarter: 15-yard touchdown run (Davis), Brown extra point.

Game Statistics

	Indianapolis	**Houston**
Total First Downs	22	17
Total Net Yards	382	273
Total Offensive Plays	65	54
Net Yards Rushing	101	148
Net Yards Passing	281	125
Passing		
Attempts-Completions-Inter.	33-26-0	21-16-1
Punts, # -Avg.	3-37.7	4-43.3
Penalties, #-yards	8-50	6-30
Touchdowns, Total	2	2
Rushing	0	1
Passing	2	1
Field Goals, made-attempts	3-3	0-0
Final Score	23	14
Time of Possession	32:19	27:41

Attendance: 70,762
Time: 3:01

Game 14

Indianapolis Colts vs.
Baltimore Ravens
December 19, 2004

Game Summary

In front of a national TV audience on ESPN, the nation watched in anticipation of Peyton Manning breaking Dan Marino's record of 48 touchdowns in a season. Indianapolis Mayor Bart Peterson announced a new stadium for the Colts that will keep them in Indianapolis for many years. Peyton didn't break the record, and the crowd wasn't happy. In the end, the ultimate goal was met — a victory — the Colts' 7th in a row.

The Colts opened the game with the ball and moved 65 yards resulting in a Mike Vanderjagt 24-yard field goal. Each team had multiple possessions in the opening quarter, with neither team making much progress. The Ravens had possession of the ball at the end of the quarter, and continued their drive into the 2nd, promptly scoring on a 42-yard field goal. COLTS 3, RAVENS 3.

The remainder of the 2nd quarter is much like the 1st, with each team having little success moving the ball toward the end zone. The quarter ends with a Mike Vanderjagt 33-yard field goal. COLTS 6, RAVENS 3.

The Ravens open the 2nd half with the ball, moving just 14 yards before having to punt. Manning and the Colts methodically move the ball toward the end zone, capping the 77-yard drive with a 29-yard touchdown pass from Manning to Marvin Harrison (**Manning's 47th of the season**). COLTS 13, RAVENS 3.

The Ravens return the kickoff for 21 yards and then go to work on offense, advancing all the way to the Colts' 13-yard line, only to have a field goal attempt blocked and advanced to the Ravens 31-yard line. After three Manning passes and two runs by Edgerrin James, the Colts are again in the end zone, after James scores from the 3-yard line. COLTS 20, RAVENS 3.

The Ravens return the kickoff for 64 yards just before the 3rd quarter comes to a close, and continue their drive into the final period. After a 36-yard field goal is nullified by a penalty, the Ravens score on a 13-yard touchdown pass from Kyle Boller to Todd Heap. Both teams exchange possessions multiple times throughout the 4th quarter, with the Colts having the final possession of the game with just under a minute remaining. Manning kneels twice to run out the clock, putting off a chance to tie Marino's record for another day, while securing a Colts victory.

COLTS 20, RAVENS 10 — FINAL.

Peyton Manning — 1 touchdown pass

Passing the Record

Dan Marino, Miami Dolphins	1984	Peyton Manning, Indianapolis Colts	2004
Opponent	TD	*Opponent*	TD
Washington	5	New England	2
New England	2	Tennessee	2
Buffalo	3	Green Bay	5
Indianapolis	2	Jacksonville	2
St. Louis	3	Oakland	3
Pittsburgh	2	Jacksonville	3
Houston	3	Kansas City	5
New England	4	Minnesota	4
Buffalo	3	Houston	5
New York	2	Chicago	4
Philadelphia	1	Detroit	6
San Diego	3	Tennessee	3
New York	4	Houston	2
Los Angeles	4	Baltimore	1
Indianapolis		San Diego	
Dallas		Denver	
Through 14 Games	**40**	**Through 14 Games**	**47**

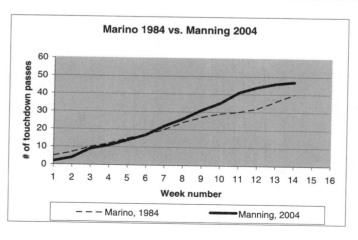

Marino 1984 vs. Manning 2004

Scoring Summary

Box Score

Team ↓ Quarter →	1	2	3	4	Score
Baltimore	0	3	0	7	10
Indianapolis	3	3	14	0	20

Baltimore

2nd Quarter: 42-yard field goal (Stover).
4th Quarter: 42-yard field goal (Stover). NULLIFIED by penalty.
13-yard touchdown pass (Boller to Heap), Stover extra point.

Indianapolis

1st Quarter: 24-yard field goal (Vanderjagt)
2nd Quarter: 33-yard field goal (Vanderjagt)
3rd Quarter: 29-yard touchdown pass (Manning to Harrison), Vanderjagt extra point.
3-yard touchdown run (James), Vanderjagt extra point.

Game Statistics

	Baltimore	Indianapolis
Total First Downs	19	17
Total Net Yards	354	316
Total Offensive Plays	71	57
Net Yards Rushing	160	67
Net Yards Passing	194	249
Passing		
Attempts-Completions-Inter.	40-19-2	33-20-0
Punts, # -Avg.	5-39.0	6-48.7
Penalties, #-yards	7-35	5-28
Touchdowns, Total	1	2
Rushing	0	1
Passing	1	1
Field Goals, made-attempts	1-2	2-3
Final Score	10	20
Time of Possession	31:22	28:38

Attendance: 57,240
Time: 3:06

Game 15

Indianapolis Colts vs.
San Diego Chargers
December 26, 2004

Game Summary

Manning has said all year that winning is more important than any individual record. On the day after Christmas, winning was foremost on Manning's mind as the Colts rallied from behind in the 4th quarter to send the game into overtime.

In the process, Manning did tie and break the record, and helped set another record as well. Brandon Stokley caught Manning's 49th touchdown pass of the season with just 56 seconds on the clock in the 4th quarter. Stokley's 10th touchdown reception of the season makes him the 3rd receiver on the team with 10 or more touchdown receptions — the first time in NFL history that a team achieved such a feat. The Colts win was overshadowed by Manning's record-breaking achievement, and Peyton Manning had a chance to talk with Dan Marino live on TV after the game.

The Chargers opened the game with the ball, and moved to their own 42-yard line before being forced to punt. The Colts took over on their 8-yard line and marched up the field to the Chargers 6-yard line, before a Manning pass intended for Reggie Wayne was intercepted. The Chargers quickly advanced the ball, moving 92-yards in 5 plays, to score on a Drew Brees 74-yard touchdown pass to La Dainian Tomlinson. The Colts' next drive extended into the 2nd quarter, ending with a 36-yard field goal by Mike Vanderjagt. COLTS 3, CHARGERS 7.

The Chargers quickly moved the ball toward the end zone, settling for a 50-yard field goal by Nate Kaeding. After a short possession by the Colts, the Chargers again took possession and headed for the end zone, with Drew Brees hitting Eric Parker for a touchdown from the 19-yard line. The Colts came back, scoring on their next two drives, with field goals by Mike Vanderjagt (26 yards and 23 yards) to end the scoring in the half. COLTS 9, CHARGERS 17.

The Colts opened the 3rd quarter with the ball, but after Manning was sacked for an 8-yard loss, Hunter Smith sent the Chargers to their own 30-yard line after a 50-yard punt. The Chargers stormed back, moving 70 yards in 9 plays to score on a 4-yard touchdown pass from Brees to Antonio Gates. COLTS 9, CHARGERS 24.

Manning brought the Colts right back, moving 72 yards in 7 plays, capping the drive with a 3-yard touchdown pass to James Mungro to **TIE THE RECORD (Manning's 48th of the season)**. The Chargers again marched up the field, taking their drive into the 4th quarter, with Tomlinson scoring on a 16-yard touchdown run. Dominic Rhodes promptly returns the kickoff 58 yards to score for the Colts. COLTS 23, CHARGERS 31.

The Chargers and Colts exchange possessions multiple times in the 4th quarter, until with just 56 seconds left in the game, Manning connects with Brandon Stokley for a 21-yard touchdown pass to bring the Colts within 2 points (**Manning's 49th of the season**). **THE RECORD HAS BEEN BROKEN!** Edgerrin James scores the 2-point conversion attempt to tie the game. COLTS 31, CHARGERS 31.

The Colts stop the Chargers' final drive in the 4th quarter and send the game to overtime, where they start with possession of the ball. Manning hits Stokley for 23 yards and Wayne for 35 yards to put them in position for a Mike Vanderjagt 30-yard field goal.

COLTS 34, CHARGERS 31 — FINAL.

Peyton Manning — 2 touchdown passes, eclipsing Marino's single-season touchdown record with one game remaining in the season

Passing the Record

Dan Marino, Miami Dolphins	1984	Peyton Manning, Indianapolis Colts	2004
Opponent	TD	*Opponent*	TD
Washington	5	New England	2
New England	2	Tennessee	2
Buffalo	3	Green Bay	5
Indianapolis	2	Jacksonville	2
St. Louis	3	Oakland	3
Pittsburgh	2	Jacksonville	3
Houston	3	Kansas City	5
New England	4	Minnesota	4
Buffalo	3	Houston	5
New York	2	Chicago	4
Philadelphia	1	Detroit	6
San Diego	3	Tennessee	3
New York	4	Houston	2
Los Angeles	4	Baltimore	1
Indianapolis	4	**San Diego**	2
Dallas		Denver	
Through 15 Games	**44**	**Through 15 Games**	**49**

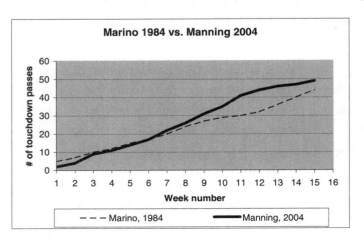

104

Scoring Summary

Box Score

Team ↓ Quarter →	1	2	3	4	OT	Score
San Diego	7	10	7	7	0	31
Indianapolis	0	9	7	15	3	34

San Diego

1st Quarter:	74-yard touchdown pass (Brees to Tomlinson), Kaeding extra point.
2nd Quarter:	50-yard field goal (Kaeding).
	19-yard touchdown pass (Brees to Parker), Kaeding extra point.
3rd Quarter:	4-yard touchdown pass (Brees to Gates), Kaeding extra point.
4th Quarter:	16-yard touchdown run (Tomlinson), Kaeding extra point.

Indianapolis

2nd Quarter:	36-yard field goal (Vanderjagt)
	26-yard field goal (Vanderjagt)
	23-yard field goal (Vanderjagt)
3rd Quarter:	3-yard touchdown pass (Manning to Mungro), Vanderjagt extra point.
	TIES THE RECORD
4th Quarter:	89-yard kickoff return for touchdown (Rhodes), Vanderjagt extra point.
	21-yard touchdown pass (Manning to Stokley), James 2-point conversion.
	BREAKS THE RECORD
OVERTIME:	30-yard field goal (Vanderjagt)

Game Statistics

	San Diego	**Indianapolis**
Total First Downs	22	30
Total Net Yards	374	464
Total Offensive Plays	61	73
Net Yards Rushing	93	104
Net Yards Passing	281	360
Passing		
Attempts-Completions-Inter.	31-21-1	44-27-1
Punts, # -Avg.	4-49.8	2-49.0
Penalties, #-yards	7-63	10-70
Touchdowns, Total	4	3
Rushing	1	0
Passing	3	2
Field Goals, made-attempts	1-1	4-5
Final Score	31	34
Time of Possession	31:13	31:34

Attendance: 57,330
Time: 3:19

Game 16

Indianapolis Colts @ Denver Broncos January 2, 2005

Game Summary

It was a game that really didn't matter. The Colts had wrapped up their spot in the playoffs. Peyton Manning had set multiple records, and everyone was looking forward to the playoffs. It was a day for the 2nd and 3rd string players to see some playing time, and for the starters to rest and prepare for the playoffs. Jim Sorgi took more snaps at quarterback today than all of the backup quarterbacks combined since Manning joined the Colts. Hunter Smith punted more times today than in any other game this season. It was a day of rest for most of the team.

It did matter to the Broncos, however, with their playoff hopes riding on this game. It was their chance to show the Colts, whom they would play next week with this day's victory, that they are a formidable opponent.

Manning starts the game and plays just the initial series. He completes one of two passes before the Colts have to punt. Manning then retires to the sidelines for the day, donning a headset and calling in plays to rookie Jim Sorgi, who has seen limited playing time this season. The Broncos are forced to punt, and Sorgi then takes the Colts 56 yards in 9 plays, scoring on a 7-yard touchdown pass to Marvin Harrison (**Sorgi's 1st of the season**). Jake Plummer and the Broncos come right back, taking just 7 plays to cover 75 yards, scoring on a 38-yard touchdown pass to Ashley Lelie. COLTS 7, BRONCOS 7.

After the Colts give the ball back to the Broncos on a punt, the Broncos score on a 45-yard field goal by Jason Elam at the beginning of the 2nd quarter. Hunter Smith is again forced to punt for the Colts, and the Broncos march back to the end zone, scoring in 10 plays on a Plummer 2-yard pass to Patrick Hape. Sorgi, with help from Manning on the sideline, sends Reggie Wayne into the end zone on a 71-yard touchdown pass (**Sorgi's 2nd of the season**), using just over 1 minute off the clock. COLTS 14, BRONCOS 17.

The 3rd quarter opens with the Broncos punting after 3 plays and the Colts doing the same on their next possession. Plummer then leads the Broncos 68 yards in 9 plays to score when he runs the ball into the end zone from the 5-yard line. After another Hunter Smith punt (he will punt 8 times today, the most of any game this season), the Broncos score on a 40-yard field goal by Jason Elam, completing the scoring in the 3rd quarter. The only score in the 4th quarter comes on another field goal by Elam, this time from 40 yards out.

COLTS 14, BRONCOS 33 — FINAL

Peyton Manning — 0 touchdown passes

Jim Sorgi — 2 touchdown passes

Passing the Record

Dan Marino, Miami Dolphins	1984	Peyton Manning, Indianapolis Colts	2004
Opponent	TD	*Opponent*	TD
Washington	5	New England	2
New England	2	Tennessee	2
Buffalo	3	Green Bay	5
Indianapolis	2	Jacksonville	2
St. Louis	3	Oakland	3
Pittsburgh	2	Jacksonville	3
Houston	3	Kansas City	5
New England	4	Minnesota	4
Buffalo	3	Houston	5
New York	2	Chicago	4
Philadelphia	1	Detroit	6
San Diego	3	Tennessee	3
New York	4	Houston	2
Los Angeles	4	Baltimore	1
Indianapolis	4	**San Diego**	2
Dallas	4	Denver	0
Through 16 Games	**48**	**Through 16 Games**	**49**

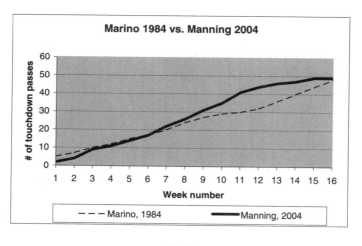

Marino 1984 vs. Manning 2004

Scoring Summary

Box Score

Team ↓ Quarter ➔	1	2	3	4	Score
Indianapolis	7	7	0	0	14
Denver	7	13	10	3	33

Indianapolis

1st Quarter:	7-yard touchdown pass (Sorgi to Harrison), Vanderjagt extra point.
2nd Quarter:	3-yard touchdown pass (Sorgi to Wayne), Vanderjagt extra point.

Denver

1st Quarter:	38-yard touchdown pass (Plummer to Lelie), Elam extra point.
2nd Quarter:	45-yard field goal (Elam)
	2-yard touchdown pass (Plummer to Hape), Elam extra point.
	23-yard field goal (Elam)
3rd Quarter:	5-yard touchdown run (Plummer), Elam extra point.
	40-yard field goal (Elam)
4th Quarter:	40-yard field goal (Elam)

Game Statistics

	Indianapolis	Denver
Total First Downs	8	23
Total Net Yards	200	453
Total Offensive Plays	43	73
Net Yards Rushing	34	214
Net Yards Passing	166	239
Passing		
Attempts-Completions-Inter.	27-17-0	30-17-0
Punts, # -Avg.	8-49.1	4-38.0
Penalties, #-yards	4-25	2-25
Touchdowns, Total	2	3
Rushing	0	1
Passing	2	2
Field Goals, made-attempts	0-0	4-4
Final Score	14	33
Time of Possession	22:16	37:44

Attendance: 75,149
Time: 3:04

Wild-Card Playoff

Indianapolis Colts vs. Denver Broncos January 9, 2005

Game Summary

The first round of the playoffs is always a motivated time for all teams. Denver had all the motivation anyone could expect: they beat the Colts the previous week to get into the playoffs and they lost badly to the Colts in this round of the playoffs last year.

The Colts and Peyton Manning had more motivation, however. The Colts came out aggressively both on offense and defense and shut down the Broncos in the 1st half. On the "road to Jacksonville", the Colts have crossed the first hurdle. Next — the Patriots in Foxboro, Mass.

The Colts opened the game with the ball and were forced to punt after just 4 plays. The Broncos did the same on their first possession. Manning and the Colts took advantage of Denver on their second drive, with a balanced running and passing attack, that ended with a **2-yard touchdown pass from Manning to James Mungro**. The Broncos punt on their next possession and the Colts waste no time in scoring again, this time on an 8-play, 87-yard drive with Edgerrin James scoring from the 1-yard line. COLTS 14, BRONCOS 0.

The Broncos open the 2nd quarter with the ball, but the Colts defense forces an interception of a Jake Plummer pass. The Colts take over on their own 41-yard line, but 5 plays later, Manning's pass to Marcus Pollard is intercepted. The Broncos are forced to punt on their next possession, giving the Colts the ball on their own 48-yard line. Four plays later, **the Colts score on a 19-yard touchdown pass from Manning to Dallas Clark**. COLTS 21, BRONCOS 0.

The Broncos score on their next possession with a 33-yard field goal by Jason Elam. An onside kick gives the Colts the ball on the Denver 40 and **the Colts score 2 plays later on a 35-yard touchdown pass from Manning to Reggie Wayne**. The Colts' defense stops the Broncos on their next possession, giving the Colts the ball with 3:13 left in the half. Manning and the Colts work the clock to score just before halftime, when Manning takes the ball into the end zone himself from the 1-yard line. COLTS 35, BRONCOS 3.

The Broncos open the 2nd half with the ball, and move 71 yards in 10 plays to score on a 9-yard touchdown pass. The Colts punt on their next possession and the Broncos march back up the field scoring in 9 plays, covering 85 yards on a 35-yard touchdown pass. COLTS 35, BRONCOS 17.

The 4th quarter opens with the Colts moving the ball up the field, again scoring when **Manning completes a 43-yard touchdown pass to Reggie Wayne**. The Broncos return the kick-off for 41 yards and score 10 plays later on a 1-yard touchdown run. The Colts answer that touchdown with one of their own, moving the ball 45 yards in 9 plays, finishing the drive with a 2-yard touchdown run by Dominic Rhodes.

COLTS 49, BRONCOS 24 — FINAL

Peyton Manning — 4 touchdown passes

Scoring Summary

Box Score

Team ↓ Quarter →	1	2	3	4	Score
Denver	0	3	14	7	24
Indianapolis	14	21	0	14	49

Denver

2nd Quarter:	33-yard field goal (Elam)
3rd Quarter:	9-yard touchdown pass (Plummer to Smith), Elam extra point.
	35-yard touchdown pass (Plummer to Putzier), Elam extra point.
4th Quarter:	1-yard touchdown run (Bell), Elam extra point.

Indianapolis

1st Quarter:	2-yard touchdown pass (Manning to Mungro), Vanderjagt extra point.
	1-yard touchdown run (James), Vanderjagt extra point.
2nd Quarter:	19-yard touchdown pass (Manning to Clark), Vanderjagt extra point.
	35-yard touchdown pass (Manning to Wayne), Vanderjagt extra point.
	1-yard touchdown run (Manning), Vanderjagt extra point.
4th Quarter:	43-yard touchdown pass (Manning to Wayne), Vanderjagt extra point.
	2-yard touchdown run (Rhodes), Vanderjagt extra point.

Game Statistics

	Denver	Indianapolis
Total First Downs	18	27
Total Net Yards	338	529
Total Offensive Plays	58	58
Net Yards Rushing	78	76
Net Yards Passing	260	453
Passing		
Attempts-Completions-Inter.	34-24-1	33-27-1
Punts, # -Avg.	4-37.5	2-38.0
Penalties, #-yards	5-24	4-25
Touchdowns, Total	3	7
Rushing	1	3
Passing	2	4
Field Goals, made-attempts	1-1	0-0
Final Score	24	49
Time of Possession	30:42	29:18

Attendance: 56,609
Time: 3:06

AFC Semifinal Playoff

Indianapolis Colts @ New England Patriots January 16, 2005

Game Summary

The Colts went to Foxboro intent on dispelling the doubters that have haunted them in the past. Peyton Manning has never won a football game in Foxboro, and this playoff game was no different. A strong New England defense, combined with dropped passes by the Colts receivers and the inability to stop the New England running game, brought much the same results as in previous meetings.

The Colts were simply outplayed, both on offense and defense. The team made no excuses and vowed to learn from the experience and come back stronger next year.

The 1st quarter was one of exchanges. The Colts opened the game with the ball but were forced to punt after just 3 plays. The Patriots went 4 plays on their first drive before having to punt. Each team went 3-and-out on its next possession, before the Colts put together a string of 7 plays, again having to punt. With 4:47 left in the 1st quarter, New England took over on its own 16-yard line and moved the ball up the field in 16 plays, covering over 9 minutes and spanning into the 2nd quarter. This Patriots drive resulted in an Adam Vinatieri 24-yard field goal. COLTS 0, PATRIOTS 3.

The Colts again go 3-and-out on their next possession, only to see the Patriots move the ball 48 yards in 6 plays resulting in another Adam Vinatieri field goal. The Colts' next possession takes them to the Patriots' 39-yard line before a fumble by Dominic Rhodes is recovered by the Patriots. The Patriots don't take advantage of the recovery and punt after 3 plays.

Manning and the Colts then move the ball 67 yards in 11 plays to end the 1st half with a Mike Vanderjagt 23-yard field goal. COLTS 3, PATRIOTS 6.

The 3rd quarter opens with the Patriots punting after just 3 plays and the Colts doing the same after a 5-play drive. The Patriots take over on their own 13-yard line and drive 87 yards in 15 plays, using over 8 minutes off the clock to score on a 5-yard touchdown pass from Tom Brady to David Givens. COLTS 3, PATRIOTS 13.

The Colts' next possession takes them into the 4th quarter, but they are again forced to punt. After a 54-yard punt by Hunter Smith, the Patriots start their next drive from their own 6-yard line. Fourteen plays and over 7 minutes later, Tom Brady runs the ball into the end zone from the 1-yard line. COLTS 3, PATRIOTS 20.

The Colts turn the ball over on a fumble by Reggie Wayne on their 2nd play of their next drive. The Patriots are forced to punt, giving the Colts one more opportunity to score with just under 3 minutes left in the game. Manning moves the ball consistently up the field, starting at his own 5-yard line. Utilizing the no-huddle offense, Manning and the Colts progress to the Patriots' 20-yard line before Manning is intercepted in the end zone with just 4 seconds left in the game.

COLTS 3, PATRIOTS 20 — FINAL

Peyton Manning — 0 touchdown passes

Scoring Summary

Box Score

Team ↓ Quarter →	1	2	3	4	Score
Indianapolis	0	3	0	0	3
New England	0	6	7	7	20

Indianapolis

2nd Quarter: 23-yard field goal (Vanderjagt)

New England

2nd Quarter: 24-yard field goal (Vinatieri)
                 31-yard field goal (Vinatieri)
3rd Quarter: 5-yard touchdown pass (Brady to Givens), Vinatieri extra point.

Game Statistics

4th Quarter: 1-yard touchdown run (Brady), Vinatieri extra point.

	Indianapolis	New England
Total First Downs	18	21
Total Net Yards	276	325
Total Offensive Plays	58	69
Net Yards Rushing	46	210
Net Yards Passing	230	115
Passing		
Attempts-Completions-Inter.	42-27-1	27-18-0
Punts, # -Avg.	6-40.7	5-39.0
Penalties, #-yards	4-44	5-35
Touchdowns, Total	0	2
Rushing	0	1
Passing	0	1
Field Goals, made-attempts	1-1	2-2
Final Score	3	20
Time of Possession	22:17	37:43

Attendance: 68,756
Time: 2:55

Index